ALL ABOUT

MONEY

To Become a Millionaire,

You Must Develop Financial Intelligence

And Learn How Money Works

2ND EDITION

MACHADO TEAM

FEB 2021

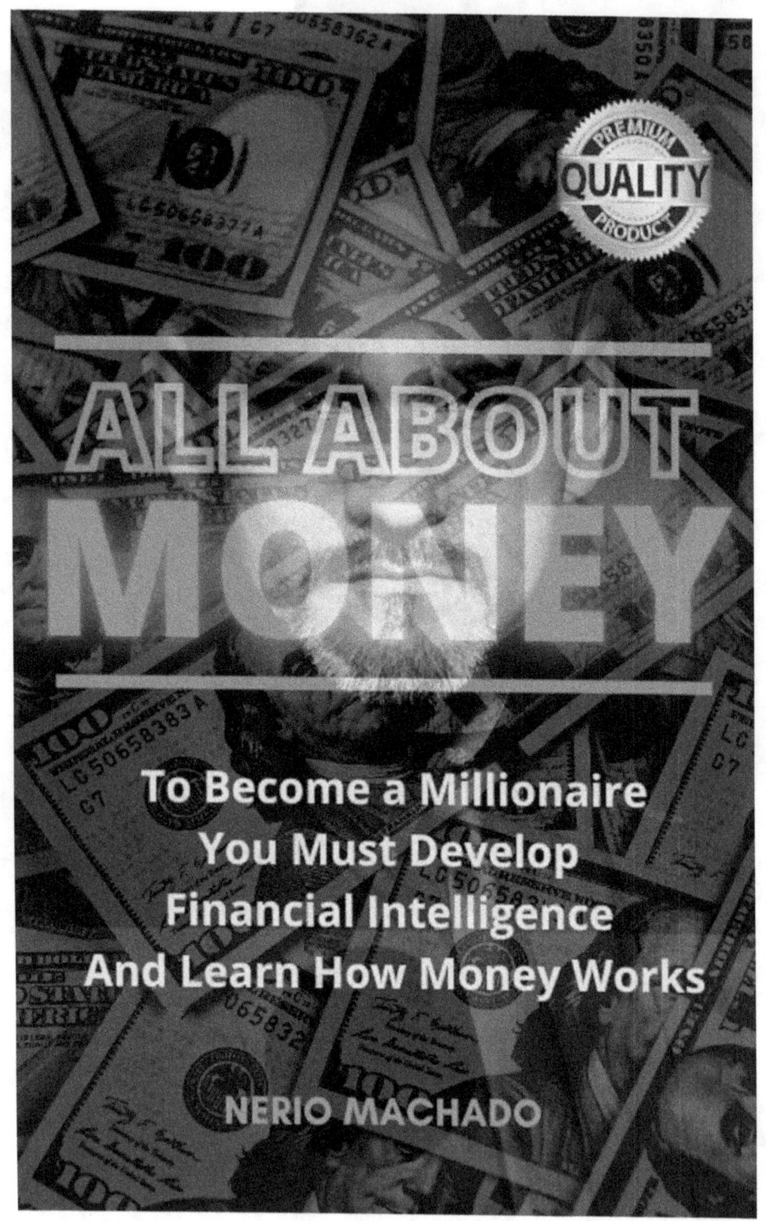
QUALITY
PREMIUM PRODUCT
ALL ABOUT MONEY
To Become a Millionaire
You Must Develop
Financial Intelligence
And Learn How Money Works
NERIO MACHADO

CONTENT

DEDICATION

To my son and daughters, Julio Cesar, Amaranta and Alana, who will be able to see that dreams come true only through effort and passion, and that each of you are capable of flying as high as you want, that each human being has the power to develop its full potential simply if it has within it a burning desire capable of burning any obstacle.

INTRODUCTION

Mayer Amschel Rothschild, founder of the Rothschild banking dynasty and father of International Finance, said: "Let me issue and create the money of a nation, and I don't care who writes the laws"

Money, you can have it or sell a lifetime to get it.

Money is everywhere, it is in the chair you are sitting on, in the cell phone you use every day, the laptop you are using, in your clothes and shoes that you like so much, also the plate in which you eat as well as the cutlery and napkins, even the vase that looks like a centerpiece, but have you ever wondered;

Where does the money come from?

How is it created?

Who controls it?

These questions seem simple, but even most economics students and professors don't know how money is created, but precisely how money is made is the main reason you can't buy a house and get a high-paying job. It is the root of the biggest problems and why there is so much complexity in the matter of money to hide the truth.

This book explains in a simple way how money and the modern monetary and banking system works.

WHERE DOES MONEY COME FROM

- complicated so you do not ask -

"Have you ever had a dream, Neo, that you were so sure it was real? What if you couldn't wake up from that dream? How would you know the difference between the world of dreams and the real world?"

The Oracle, The Matrix

In our modern economy we have two types of money; paper money and electronic money, the latter being the most commonly used today. Electronic money is the numbers you see in your account or your card's payment for when you go shopping. If we think of money in terms of everyday use there will not be much difference between these two types of money, if for example you buy a cup of coffee and pay with your credit or debit card or do it in cash, the difference seems to be more Well a matter of preference, however, if we ask ourselves about how money is created, then we see that there is a big difference with paper and electronic money.

The Central Bank creates paper money in the form of bills or coins and if someone else tries to make it they would be jailed for counterfeiting. Many people believe that the Central Bank is the main organization that creates money. In reality, only 3% to 5% of the total money supply is created by the Central Bank. The remaining 95% to 97% is electronic money created by the commercial banks. What happens is that electronic money is very intricate.

Many people believe that electronic money is just the electronic version of paper money, but that is not true. Electronic money is created by commercial banks when they issue new loans. Imagine that you go to the bank to obtain a loan of $ 10,000.00 and this loan is rarely paid with cash, it happens that when you spend electronic money you simply transfer it from your bank account or to someone else's bank account, and this process makes the electronic money is not transferred on paper, but the transfer is made electronically. For example, when a bank issues a loan of $ 1,000,000.00 it means that the bank simply creates and adds that million dollars to the economy's total money supply.

I suppose you must be wondering right now, where the hell did that bank get a million dollars to make the loan?, Could it be that an army of old men who kept their life savings in the bank for years and the bank took them from there to execute the loan? Well the answer is; NOT. What happened is that the bank only wrote numbers in your account, and I explain you in steps;

Step 1: you sign the loan.

Step 2: the bank writes numbers to your account.

That's it, and the result is that 95% to 97% of the money supply is created this way

And now I am sure that you are saying that this is impossible. There is no way that the bank can simply write electronic numbers in an account when a loan is requested, but it is. And I leave you a quote issued by the same Central Bank of England; "Commercial banks create money in the form of deposits through new loans, for example, for someone applying for a housing loan. He does not do it by giving him thousands of bills, but they credit that amount in his bank account. At that moment money is created."

You get excited about all the innovative ways out there to make payments with payment cards and smartphones, but we have to remember the price we pay for such convenience. We have essentially privatized the creation of money in our society. You've surely heard the saying; "Money is power", if money is power then what does it mean to give the creation of this power to the banks that are for-profit organizations?

Now you have realized then the great problem that it means to let the banks create money from nothing. It is not that we now hate banks, it is not about that, nor that banks are the bad guys of the game and the bankers are greedy and unscrupulous, the issue is to recognize how much power has been given to the banking industry.

We have allowed them to combine two vital processes, money creation and money lending. As a result when banks lend money they are creating money. It is very important to understand this issue because it directly impacts you, it is the main reason why you cannot buy a house or have a good job. Like any business, banks also want to maximize their profits and minimize their risks, which means that they have incentives to lend money to certain sectors that are less risky, and guess which is the sector with the lowest risk for banks, I already know you know, the real estate sector. For banks it is risky to lend money to small companies because there is a high probability that they will not have to pay back the loan and the interest, because they can fail and declare themselves in the bank, in reality the success rate is low, unlike mortgages which They have security, since if the loan applicant has no way to pay, the mortgage is simply foreclosed. The bank keeps the property to cover its losses.

Therefore, it makes a lot of sense for banks to lend money through mortgages then the newly created money flows into the real estate market instead of flowing or being directed to other sectors that society needs, such as; new businesses, schools, hospitals, police, fire departments, parks, etc. The most incredible thing is that at first glance it may seem that society benefits from cheap mortgages, but it is not like that, because imagine that "Santa Claus" appears on Christmas Eve and doubles or triples the amount of money that everyone has, So if you had $ 10,000.00 in your bank account, you would have $ 30,000.00 and surely now with that false feeling that everyone is rich they would run to the stores to spend all that money, and what happens next is that all prices start to go up, and since all prices go up, no one would benefit. Therefore, the same effect is the one that occurs on real estate, which is contrary to what most people believe or are made to believe by the same system, since the false belief is that house prices rise due to migration, population increase, decrease in the number of houses built. Although these factors play a role, they are not the main reason for the rise in house prices.

The biggest reason comes from the impact of the increase in mortgage loans in 10 years, for example, between 1997 and 2007 in the United States it was 40% of the money just created was destined to the real estate market, 37% the financial markets and 3% to credit cards and personal loans, and only 13% went to commercial loans that are those that benefit the economy. Those dangerous real estate bubbles are those that explode from one day to the next leaving many people unprotected and at risk of losing their homes for not knowing how money works and consequently without being able to predict or perceive a debacle of this type, such as the one that It happened in 2008 after that previous 10-year period injecting money into the real estate sector by the banking system.

This book has been written in the year 2020 and at this time a similar bubble is being reached. The times may be shorter because the amount of money that banks inject into the flow of circulating money is increasing by the obvious need for more people entering the home buying stage. That is why on average house prices rise 7% while wages increase only 0.8%. This situation is very similar worldwide, as you can see almost 80% of the money went to non-productive sectors that do not benefit the economy or job creation. As a result no new jobs are created and unemployment increases. For example, in Italy 40% of young people under 25 are unemployed, in Spain it is 56%, in Greece 60%, this is alarming and in turn is a massive waste of talented people who want to do something useful with their lives, but they can't, simply because of how money is created and distributed in the modern monetary system. So if you want to solve the problem of unemployment and the acquisition of housing, you must know how our money is created.

One of the common questions in the midst of all this is that if banks have created so much money because we do not have inflation in the economy, then as you have just seen, a large part of the newly created money does not flow to the economy but to the real estate market and financial, therefore inflation is created in the direction where the money flows, and that is why the prices of houses and stocks are rising while the rest of the economy moves very slowly.

Years ago, a member of the family worked. He could only support the family and buy a house, but today, both work and cannot buy a house. Many young families who qualify for mortgages can barely afford their regular expenses and mortgage payments, and what if the interest on the mortgages increases, as the banks take the houses, and here comes the most important question, what the bank asked to have the right to take away the houses of these people, if what you did was write numbers on a computer screen adding those numbers in your account, creating money without backup? Incredible, a great deal for banks, which is why mortgages are the best-selling product on the shelves of all banks, so it is a bad idea to let the banks create money and control it.

Instead of getting excited about all these new innovative and electronic forms of payment, think for a moment who benefits from all this, because since everything is electronic, banks are closing branches, closing ATMs, reducing their workforce. They no longer need to buy armored cars to transport the money. All this translates into lower costs for the banks, in addition to the massive and abrupt profits they obtain by creating money from nothing, that is, realize that all these electronic, innovative, and All those financial instruments that are created to make your life easier, as well as using your smartphone as an electronic payment card, wireless points of sale, payment web pages, *Ecommerce* pages, credit card processing websites, etc., have designed to circulate money faster and get it out of your pocket or your virtual bank account faster.

Let's now look at 3 more problems that our banking system has; inequality, instability and power in the hands of a small group of people.

Let's start with the instability, the way the banks lend money is very similar to an umbrella store that sells umbrellas when the sun rises but when it starts to rain the store closes, now when the economy is booming stocks and prices Housing prices begin to rise and at that time the banks are interested in lending money to inject it into the economy, however, that inflates the prices of the economy even more and we know ultimately these bubbles explode as we already mentioned what happened in the 2008, and there begins a crisis.

And guess what? When crises occur, banks become reluctant to lend money and put it into circulation in the economy and this makes the situation worse, that is, if you are a good observer, banks are in charge and benefit from creating money to lend you when they are not. needs, but it is when you are more willing to request it because you feel confident and sure that you can handle it or face the debt, but the truth is that most people do not have financial intelligence and are not prepared to face a crisis, since They do not have reserves or assets, just a simple and basic way to earn money through a job that when a crisis comes is the main affected sector since most companies begin to reduce staff to reduce operational costs while they exceed the crisis.

The second problem, Inequality, and as it is well known when we lend money we must pay interest on that loan and we can think of this interest as a kind of tax on money, however this tax works in a way contrary to normal taxes, since In the normal tax system where the more money you earn the more taxes you will pay, however in the banking world the more you earn the richer you are the less taxes you will pay, in other words, the richer you are and the more active you have the less interest you pay. On the other hand, if you are poor and have little money, you will have to pay a high interest rate. The way money is created is a clear explanation of the inequality in our society and why it is continuing to increase. The same inequality also applies to countries, for example, some countries pay high interest rates, therefore, they get poorer and poorer, while other countries get richer and richer and pay interest rates every year. lower times.

The third problem is about Power, if you can decide "when" to create money, if you can say "how much" new money to create, if you can decide how much "interest" to charge, if you can decide for what "purpose" to lend the money, then you have enormous power over others and this power is not only over the economy but also over society, so having practically privatized the way of creating money we have at the same time given enormous power to the banks. That is why many politicians today seem very powerless because crucial decisions are not made in Parliament, they are made in the boardroom of the major private banking corporations.

We need to start questioning the power we have given to the banks, we need to start asking ourselves if we need a big banking industry, while other sectors like healthcare, schools and small businesses suffer.

A common thing to hear is that debt is bad but money is good, and people want money but do not want debt, and they do not understand that this is not possible, and that is that in the current system money is equal to debt, and if we want more money, then we have to acquire more debt, and if no one gets into debt then the economy will not move, and if there is no money spending will decrease and when spending goes down basically the economy also goes down, and that is why you listen on the television that politicians talk about paying the debt but they do not realize how ridiculous it sounds when they make these statements, unfortunately most people do not understand about money and how it works and they believe all that circus.

We spend our whole life trying to earn money, we use it every day, but we are not informed about it, people do not want to talk about it because they think it is taboo, think money is bad. Money is not good or bad. Money is bad because pizza is bad, it all depends on how you use the money, because with it you can build a hospital or build an atomic bomb. Society has so many problems simply because of ignorance about money. I believe that if enough people are informed, positive changes can occur.

HOW MONEY WORKS

- your financial success depends on this –

"If we could first know where we are and where we are going, we could better judge what to do and how to do it."

Abraham Lincoln

They say money doesn't grow on trees, but the truth is that the modern banking system creates currency much faster than the time it takes for trees to grow, most people have no idea how currency is created, economists and bankers can make it look so complex that people think they can't figure it out, but I'm going to strip our monetary system so you can see the scam behind the curtain and how it affects you.

Every modern society creates currencies in the same way, but since the US dollar is the most widely used world currency, we will use the United States as an example to explain the monetary system.

It all starts when a politician says, "vote for me and I'll make sure to give you more free stuff than my opponent", but free lunches don't exist, so to provide those supposedly free things politicians make sure the country spends more money than your income and this is called deficit spending.

To pay for this deficit spending, the treasury borrows foreign currency by issuing a bond, but then what is a bond? A bond is nothing more than a big "I Owe You", and an "I Owe You" is a nice piece of paper with numbers printed on it that says "Lend Me A Million Dollars Today and I Promise During the 10-Year Period I Will Pay Back Million Dollars plus Interest ", but what you need to understand is that treasury bonds are our national debt, and you, me and our descendants will repay these large promissory notes through future taxes, therefore, when the Government issues a bond it steals the prosperity of the future to be able to spend it today, and the way this system works is like this;

Step 1: The Government creates large promissory notes, these bonds increase our national debt and make citizens pay it.

Step 2: The I Owe You are exchanged to create currency, the Treasury sells the bonds to the banks, then the banks turn around and sell our national debt at a profit to the Federal Reserve, which is the Central Bank of the United States. from America. The Federal Reserve then opens its checkbook that doesn't have a penny on the dollar and buys those bond notes that it writes and checks into a checking account that has a balance of "Zero", then they give those checks to the banks and the coin just pops up and then the whole process repeats.

This results in an accumulation of Federal Reserve bonds and Treasury currency which is just a supply of numbers. The Treasury deposits the newly created currency in the various branches of Government and the politicians say, "Thank you very much", finally the government makes a deficit spending on public works, salaries, social programs and war, later government employees, contractors and the military deposit their pay in the banks. Now this may come as a surprise to you but when they deposit their money in the bank they are not actually depositing in an account to keep it safe, instead you are lending the bank your money and within the legal limits they can do with it just about anything they want, this includes betting it on the Stock Market or lending it to a beneficiary and earning interest, of course now this is where the currency creation machine kicks in, because this is where something called "Fractional Reserve Loans"

The fractional reserve loan is exactly what it says, banks are allowed to reserve only a fraction of your deposit and withdraw the rest. Although reserve ratios may vary we will use a reserve ratio of 10% as an example; If you deposit 100 dollars in your account, the bank can legally take 90 dollars and lend it without notifying you, the Bank must retain 10 dollars from your reserve in case you want something from it, these reserves are called "Box Cash" but because your bank account It still says that you have $ 100. The bank has stolen $ 90 from you? Well, the bank left something called bank credit in your account instead of those $ 90 or what is the same, another type of I Owe You. Now I know this sounds crazy but here's the black and white of the Federal Reserve, commercial banks create money in the checkbook when they make loans by simply adding new deposit dollars to their book accounts in exchange for IOUs from the Borrower, these are nothing more than numbers that banks type in their computers. Although these I Owe You bank credit numbers are very different from the base currency numbers it is still money, so now there are 190 dollars.

Now, the reason people borrow from banks is to buy something they want, like a house or a car or something like that, then the borrower takes the $ 90 from your account and pays the seller of the item. The seller deposits that currency into his account, and his bank lends 90% of that and leaves the bank credit numbers in place, so now there is $ 271 in stock. Guess what? This process is repeated and repeated until under a reserve ratio of 10% an initial deposit of only 100 dollars can create up to 1000 dollars of bank credit and all backed by 100 dollars of safe, only 10%, but as I said Reservation fees vary greatly and on some 10% deposits can vary to 3% of the deposit, but in other cases the reservation requirements are 0%. So once again when the currency is deposited in the banks the banks can lend it and then it is re-deposited and lent and deposit and lend and deposit and lend over and over again creating bank credit entirely.

This is where the vast majority of our currency supply comes from, in fact 92% to 96% of all existing currency is not created by the government but here in the banking system, now the massive amounts of currency that flow into society can It may seem like a fun idea at first, but you must remember one of the most important hidden secrets of money; The prices of goods and services act like a sponge in an expanding currency, the more currencies we have, the more prices will rise, and this is where inflation comes from, that is, inflation is an expansion of the money supply and the increase in prices is simply the symptom. Our entire supply of currency is nothing, but a couple of bucks generate in this scam the center of everything where the treasury and the federal reserve exchange glorified the I Owe You and a bunch of numbers that banks just they write on their computers.

That's our full currency supply, it's nothing more than a supply of numbers, some of them, most of them typed and there's nothing else, but if you thought it was crazy get ready for a dark zone of the modern economy, we work for a part of currency supply where the true wealth is your time because we trade moments in our lives, hour for hour, day to day and year to year for numbers that someone simply typed on a computer and now those numbers represent our blood, sweat and tears, work and talent. We are what gives the currency value, but here comes the really cruel joke, we work hard to be able to save some of that money so that we can pay the tax collector that in the United States is known as the IRS who then delivers it to the Treasury so that the Treasury can pay the principal plus the interest on that bond that the Federal Reserve bought with a check written from an account that has nothing inside, is empty, is at zero.

Now let's do a summary and pay close attention because this is where the system starts robbing you and me on a grand scale; Much of our taxes are not used for schools, roads and public services but to pay interest on the bonds that the Federal Reserve bought with a check written in an account that has nothing, it is at "zero", it has no support anymore that the military might of the United States to enforce its currency globally, therefore, the Federal Reserve is committing fraud, but here is one of the biggest secrets of all, something that most of the common citizen is unaware of, and that is that Before the creation of the Federal Reserve there was no need for Personal Income Tax, that is, people were not required to pay a tax for goods and services acquired. The Federal Reserve was created in 1913. That same year the Constitution was modified to allow for Income Tax, and do you think this was just a coincidence? Ask yourself the following question; How much income tax have you paid all your life? Well, much of this has been quietly diverted into the hands of those who own the system, yes! As we have said before, this system has owners, and who those owners are is the biggest secret that we will reveal shortly, but first we must understand the so-called "debt ceiling".

Everything is based on a great paradox, interest was owed on those bonds and interest was also owed on those loans that banks made, that means that there is interest owed for every dollar in existence, and let me ask you something, if you borrow the first dollar that exists and is the only one that exists on the planet, but you promise to return it plus other dollars as interest, where do you get the second dollar to pay the interest? The answer is that you must borrow that product and promise to pay it with interest as well, so now there are 2 dollars, but you owe 4 dollars and so on. The result of this spiral of money is that there is never enough money to pay the debt there is always more debt in existence than money in the system, therefore, the whole system is impossible, it is finite and will come to an end one day.

What would happen if the Government stopped borrowing to make deficit spending, will the payments of those bonds be taken from the treasury? What would happen if the public stops borrowing and borrowing more? Will your house and car payments stop? Well the answer is no, because there is a payment due each month on the principal plus interest on each existing dollar and those payments do not stop, if we stop borrowing then a new currency is not created to replace the currency we use to Making those payments, whether you're making a loan payment or paying taxes to make a bond payment - the portion of the payment that goes toward paying principal extinguishes that part of the debt, but the debt also extinguishes the currency. Currency and debt are like matter and antimatter, when they meet they destroy each other.

If we only pay the principal of all the loans and bonds that exist, the entire money supply simply disappears, so if we don't go deep into the debt every year, see what happens; everything collapses into a deficit collapse under the weight of those payments. That's why politicians like to talk about balancing the budget by paying off debt and living within our means, and saying they love it because it makes them sound so smart and in reality they just repeat what a smart and astute economist adviser whispers in their ear. , but in reality they do not understand that this is deflationary, it is impossible to do it under our current monetary system without collapsing the entire economy, therefore they never do it, they only say it to look smart in front of the cameras and appear to be an absolute and decisive solution to the suffocation the population's financial debt, because talking about a debt ceiling is not just ridiculous, it is delusional, because the system is designed to require increasing levels of debt just to continue, and that is why politicians always postpone the problem and raise that so-called debt ceiling until the day finally comes when everything collapses under its weight. In other words, they don't want it to crash on their clock, America's founding fathers knew the dangers of central banking and wanted to fight to break free from it. Thus came the revolutionary war, which began as a tax revolt, and this most do not know, and that is that the people were asphyxiated from paying ever higher taxes, to build and create everything we know today as a nation, but now we must pay taxes just to have a monetary system.

Having suffered from the hyperinflation of the continental dollar that was forgotten to finance the revolutionary war, they understood the dangers of fiat currency and debt-based monetary systems, then to protect future generations from institutional and government theft, they wrote in the Constitution that only gold and silver can be money, for the simple fact that they cannot be printed. Our current system is not only unconstitutional, it robs us of our freedom and prosperity. We are all feeling the effects of ignoring the Constitution at this time, since by forcing the circulation of more currency our purchasing power is diluted, inflation is a stealth, slow and insidious tax that simply the result of a monetary system based on the department. This system empowers and benefits those who create the currency and receive it first as they can spend it in circulation before it affects the economy. They are stealing purchasing power from us and transferring it to the banks and the Government every hour of every day due to this false monetary system, and it is not that the people above do not know this, here is a sample that the information is public knowledge It's just that 95% of people don't understand or understand and don't care about learning economics, so here's a quote from the Federal Reserve; "The decrease in purchasing power incurred by money holders due to inflation imparts profits to money issuers"

This is a real fraud. It is a pyramid scheme, a Ponzi scheme, a scam, and our entire monetary system is a lie. It is nothing more than a form of legalized theft, but this is the biggest problem of all. The Federal Reserve is not federal, it has shareholders, there is no federal agency that has shareholders, but what is a shareholder?

A share represents a percentage of a corporation's ownership, so the shareholders are the owners of that corporation. Therefore, the Federal Reserve is a private corporation with owners. You can see it for yourself if you visit the Federal Reserve website and it will say, "Shareholders receive a 6% annual dividend."

Now we know that the Federal Reserve shares were originally issued to the largest banks in the United States, but due to mergers and acquisitions over the years it cannot be traced who owns the Federal Reserve shares, It is a very well-kept secret. I suppose the owners are the main traffickers, the banks that make a profit by selling part of our national debt from those Federal Reserve bonds that buy them with a check from nowhere, then we pay taxes to pay the principal and interest on their bonds so the Federal Reserve can pay the banks a 6% dividend.

Don't be alarmed if you don't understand the deception of this system at first glance, very few people do, it is deliberately complex. The economist John Maynard King once wrote; "In this way, the Government can confiscate the people's wealth in secret and without being observed. No man in a million would recreate the theft."

If presented correctly, anyone can understand the system, regardless of how complex it is. This system is fundamentally evil, it channels the wealth of the workforce to the government and the banking sector, it is the cause of the artificial booms and busts of the modern economy and it causes a great wealth disparity between the rich and the working class. It is only possible because we no longer use money we make foreign currency. Still, worst of all it is a form of slavery since every time a Government issued a bond, it promises to make us pay taxes in the future. Nobody asked you if you wanted to pay imposed today by the prosperity, we all enjoyed in the last century. No one has asked our children if they want to work hard tomorrow for the supposed prosperity, we all enjoy today.

George Washington wrote once; "No generation has the right to incur debts greater than those that can be paid in the course of its existence."

By stealing tomorrow's prosperity so we can spend it today, we enslave ourselves and future generations. This all sounds bad enough, but there is great hope. You are the biggest threat to this false monetary system. This system depends on the public ignoring its operation. Share this knowledge with everyone you know, because an informed public that fully understands the system can build a better future for generations to come.

And now I leave you with this quote attributed to a former director of the Bank of England;

"The modern banking system makes money out of thin air; the process is perhaps the most amazing sleight of hand ever invented. The bank was conceived in iniquity and was born in sin. The bankers own the land, take it away from them, but give them the power to create money and control credit and with just a pen they will create enough money to buy it back. If you want to continue as a slave to the bankers and pay the cost of your slavery, let them continue to create money and control credit".

HIDDEN SECRETS ABOUT MONEY

- the rich don't want you to know this -

"We live in a world where the truth is overshadowed by a reality that does not exist."

Albert Einstein

Your true wealth is your time and your freedom. Money is just a tool to exchange your time. It is a container to store your economic energy until you are ready to deploy it, but the whole world has been turned away from real money. Now it has been tricked into using currency, a deceptive imposter who is silently stealing your most valuable assets; your time and your freedom.

Today we are entering a period of financial crisis, possibly the greatest the world has ever known. The wealth transfer that will take place during this decade is the largest wealth transfer in history. Wealth is never destroyed it is simply transferred, that means that on the opposite side of every crisis there is an opportunity, the good news is that all you have to do to turn this crisis into your great opportunity is to educate yourself, I think the best investment what you can do in your life is your education; education about the history of money, education about finance, education about money and how the global economy works. If you keep up to date with what is happening and how the financial world works, you can put yourself on the right side of wealth transfer.

Wiston Churchill once said, "The more you look at the past, the more you can see into the future," and what I wish is that you can create your crystal ball. One of the main reasons we are in the financial mess we have today globally is that people do not understand the difference between currency and money. Currency is a medium of exchange, a unit of account, it is portable, durable, visible and something called ingible. It means that each unit is equal to the next dollar unit, but this we had already mentioned before. A dollar in my pocket buys the same amount as a dollar in your pocket.

Money is all those things plus a store of value over a long period, even financial planners, bankers, your accountant don't understand the difference between currency and money. The currency in a pocket is a medium of exchange it is a unit of account because it has numbers, it is something durable, portable and can do exchange, but because governments can print more and more and dilute the supply of currency, that means that wealth is transferred from your pocket, from your bank account to the government and the banking system.

This is why governments and cowboys assemble paper money, because it is very easy to manipulate the money supply and steal wealth. They don't like that money is handled through gold and silver, because they can't print it.

The reason why gold and silver are the optimal form of money is due to their properties, it is an easy medium of exchange because gold and silver store a large amount of value in a very small area, it is a unit of account. Pure gold has the same value all over the planet, so an ounce of gold buys the same amount in Spain, China, the United States and Venezuela. Gold and silver are durable, the same gold that Egyptians used in trade 5000 years ago is still here with us today, it does not corrode, it is divisible, you can make changes with it, it is very portable, you can use something like the Oil as money, but you cannot carry a barrel of oil to buy things, it is expendable.

Pure gold is the same anywhere on earth, pure silver the same anywhere on earth, but it is limited in quantity and that is why it maintains its purchasing power, governments cannot print it. In the last 5000 years, only gold and silver have maintained their purchasing power. There have been thousands and thousands of fiat currencies. If you don't know the fiat currency is paper money.

History shows that currencies that are not backed by gold or silver have been reduced to zero, it is a 100% failure rate, let me repeat it, there is not a single paper money in history that has not reached zero Do you think that the Dollar, the Euro or the Peso will not happen to them the same? And it is that no fiat currency has survived. The fiat currency is a currency that exists at the government's dictation. They have the printing presses and they print it. Then they use a fiat allocation that makes the currency official, but in reality it is only worthless paper. The Central Bank of America is very open about what they are doing, if you read their website it says there is no intrinsic value in your money, they tell you that they print it backed by absolutely nothing, but you do tell someone in public that money is created out of nothing and that there is no absolute endorsement, that it has no value, that it is as valuable as monopoly money, they will look at you like you are crazy.

There is a well-accepted definition of what money is, the question is, does circulating money fit the definition that people know? well just take the paper dollar for example and ask yourself if it performs those functions, does it store value? the dollar has lost 95% of its purchasing power since the Federal Reserve's creation in 1913. therefore, it is not very good as a store of value.

A very curious experiment that I have seen is one where there are 3 images, one of them is a pile of monopoly money, the other is a pile of Federal Reserve notes what Americans call paper money. The other is solid gold, then people are asked which of these is not like the other. This has been done with groups of university professors. It has also been shown to children. When the professors clearly say that the Dolores are not like the others because gold does not have the role as money and monopoly money is false. The dollar American is a store of value. Still, the kids look at it and say that gold is not like the others. The other two are paper and gold, so my question is who is smarter, a university professor or 5 years old?

Before World War I, each note issued by the US Treasury endorsed $ 20 in gold coins payable to the bearer upon request, the money remained in the vault. The money or currency was a note represented with a claim check, just a check claim on the money, that is, the same as if you go to the dry cleaner and leave your shirt. They give you a receipt as a guarantee of your shirt until you go for it and claim it again, the value is really in the shirt not in the receipt that says that you are the owner of the shirt, in conclusion the money was just a claim check, that's why the second hidden secret is the difference between currency and money.

Money must be a store of value and maintain its purchasing power for long periods. National currencies are a tool used by the Government and the financial sector to steal your time and freedom, stealing your purchasing power, so instead of storing your economic energy the currencies escape, now compare that with the gold and silver that used by the Egyptians, that is, people are amazed to see that the pyramids are still here. Those people used trade to build pyramids that still exist, that gold could have been melted and refined and be present in a coin or a bar or some piece of jewelry, but you are still with us today. You still buy something, you can buy things, that's why it is definitive money, divisible. It is permanent, it is a store of value, it is a unit of account, it has everything you want from money, it does not disappear and cannot be increased, that is what makes gold the most beautiful money of all, what more can you ask money for? The value of this mineral keeps governments in check. That's why they don't like gold, because they are getting away with fiat currencies. They will do everything they can to discredit it as an asset class, it is the fear that perhaps gold will prevail over the system and limit the government's ability to spend beyond its means.

You probably know that inflation is an expansion of the money supply as already indicated above and that deflation is a contraction of the money supply, therefore, if you expand the money supply eventually prices will rise and if you contract the supply of foreign exchange eventually prices will fall. This is a pool, but it is not a pool of water, it is a pool of foreign exchange, and if you expand the supplies of foreign exchange the prices like a sponge in the water must rise to absorb the excess foreign exchange. Now, governments never stop increasing the circulation of currency, therefore, prices continue to rise, it is not because the things you are trying to buy are changing, real estate does not change, what has changed is the purchase of currency every lower time, is the currency going down, house prices do not rise.

Before we had a currency, we had TRADE; I give you 3 coconuts and you give me 4 fish because it is a fair exchange, but that got complicated, that's why we had to invent this thing called money to be a portable and divisible medium of exchange and the challenge is that we have lost that long ago time, we lost having things of value like our currency and now we have this thing called numbers and accounts, but I repeat, it is not real money, it is a great invented story, a story called "Quantitative Expansion" that makes it look very complex, but that's just a confusing term, a smoke screen and mirrors for currency creation.

Quantitative easing started with bank bailouts in 2009, this currency was created out of thin air and then given to banks to pay record bonds in reward for collapsing the world economy. This is a global phenomenon, but you must remember now that those terms of RESCUE or STIMULATION PROGRAMS are just "troublemakers" terms for further currency creation. Many people think that they will be fine in their country, that this will only happen in the United States or maybe in Europe, but what they do not realize is that it is a global phenomenon.

I have to show you something here, when the dollar as such was created was a circulating amount in line with the number of people and businesses at the time, but in a matter of 200 years it went from having practically no dollars in existence to $ 825 million, and then we had bailouts and then we had quantitative easing and then we had quantitative easing 2nd and then 3rd and then 4th and soon we'll have 57 and 380 and it's not just how it looks in the United States, it's also how it looks in Canada, so it is in Australia, South Africa and Russia, also in Singapore, it is the same story, all the governments on the planet are doing this crazy supply spending and expanding their supplies of currency, doing financial bailouts and history shows that there is no example of let this go well.

Surprisingly, we have not experienced more inflation than we do. We continue to expand the money supply so widely because prices are not growing faster than they are. The answer is that a good part of the money that created the system of Federal Reserve has been sent abroad.

Surely you have heard that Americans have exported their inflation, because when I heard it I could not understand it, how is that? How can you export your inflation? Put a box on it and send it how do you do with a pair of shoes? Well now I understand that because inflation is exported simply by sending all those dollars that you created to other countries, they send you refrigerators and their cars, their televisions. Hence, you get physical things and they have small pieces of paper. It's big business for the American people for a while, but sooner or later all those dollars will come home and when the time comes, and I assure you that time is near, because the rest of the world will say they don't want to play that game anymore. Uncle Sam's dollars that don't have that much value anymore and they will want something more than US dollars. Right there those dollars will start coming back to the United States and people will say "we don't want them anymore".

Once the rain of money that the United States has exported for years begins to return, the previous inflation will also pick up. Then we will see that the amount of money within the United States will grow much faster. During the second round of quantitative expansion world food prices rose 160% and this created a humanitarian disaster for the millions of people on earth who lived on less than $ 2 a day, these people were hungry. They became hungrier and began to overthrow their governments in North Africa and around the Middle East.

Quantitative easing was the spark that ignited the Arab Spring. When you create money, you get some kind of inflation, it just depends on where the inflation goes. Inflation mainly affects people in the percentage of their income that goes to food and we see this as a relationship and we know that there are some danger points, for example, in Egypt once that proportion reached 40% of the income destined to food and the price of food began to rise due to inflation, people started a revolution. That is exactly what we saw similarly in the French revolution, which relied on food price to reach a certain critical point where the risk reward for the revolution was favorable towards the revolution.

When there is an inflation index, the people who are more productive in society are being punished, in other words, the people who produce more than they consume and save the difference, the problem is that those productive people, the savers save in your national currency and unfortunately the national currency is just a sheet of fiat paper right now, so when it gets destroyed through inflation, those $ 100,000.00 you were hoping to retire with no longer exists, and the things you were going to buy with that money does not exist either.

Now what are you going to do? That seems scary; however, you know this will happen and you can only play the dealing hand, but the great news is that gold and silver always end up accounting for the expansion of currency supplies. When governments do these kinds of things to the money supply, inflation finally returns when they degrade it. People feel the loss of their purchasing power, they rush to return to gold and silver and offer the value of gold and silver in the country until it reaches or exceeds the value of all currency in circulation, this is a process that has been happening repeatedly throughout history except this time it is happening on a global scale, it has never happened in all countries at once before and that means this is the largest transfer of wealth in history, therefore it is the best chance ever and it won't happen again in your life.

Now we have learned that your true wealth is your time and freedom. Money is a negotiation tool that stores the economic energy that is your time and your freedom while currencies escape this monetary energy. Gold and silver are the ultimate money simply because of their properties, fiat currencies are based solely on trust and always return to their third intrinsic value. Governments don't like gold because it imposes moderation. Rising prices is an expanding money supply system and gold and silver always accompany an expanding money supply. For now my challenge for you is to stop calling currency money which is a crucial first step to free your mind from all the confusion and economic plot and change your context.

FINANCIAL CRISIS

- understand it and get over it -

"It is already well known that the people of this nation do not understand anything about our banking and monetary system, if they did, I think there would be a revolution before tomorrow morning."

Henry Ford

The next economic crisis is approaching it has already started its first phase and it will be progressive and sustained and if you want to understand the situation and prepare to face it and overcome it, you should pay close attention to this chapter from the beginning to the end.

We are going to walk through several ideas and analysis of Robert Kiyosaki, who for most does not have a presentation, however, we can add here that Kiyosaki is a recognized Guru of personal finance and real estate, and also was one of the few people who correctly predicted the financial crisis of 2008.

During a crisis wealth is not destroyed, it is simply transferred from one group to another. If you study history you can predict the future and prepare correctly, that is why we are going to divide the thread of time into 3 blocks: past, present and future.

Let's start with the past. History repeats itself over and over again, governments simply refuse to learn its lessons, and to understand the past, two important terms must be taken into account, the first is the

Quantitative Expansion and the second, the Gold Standard under the Bretton woods agreement.

Let's start with quantitative easing, it simply means printing money, you may wonder why we don't just call it printing money? Well, I guess governments usually use complex terms so that average people don't understand what is happening. If you have financial problems and decide to print money in your basement then you will be arrested if you are discovered, however, the Government does something very similar without anyone saying anything. Governments generally print money when they are in economic crisis or when the money is needed for critical situations, such as war.

Why is printing money bad? The answer is that every time money is printed, poor people and the middle class get poorer, and it seems that the rich in turn get richer. Printing money destroys the value of money, increases inflation and taxes, the wealth of ordinary people is stolen through inflation. Inflation is certainly bad for the average person; it means that the money they have worked hard to earn is suddenly less valuable. Printing money is not a new trick, governments have used it for several centuries and the scary thing is that they always ended in disaster, no evidence in history shows that printing money has brought long-term prosperity. The printing of money directs poor people and an even larger government governed by political forces rather than true economic laws. We can cite hundreds of modern examples from this century, but I like to penetrate history to realize that it is always the same in different contexts of time. So, let's take the Roman Empire, because the further you look back the further you can see into the future, so when the Roman Empire faced war they started to corrupt the currency, which is equivalent to printing money. What the Romans did to increase the flow of circulating currency is that since silver and gold were used as money they began to melt it down and mix it with other metals, they also tried another version of money printing called coin clipping, which means that When the tax money was collected they cut the edges of the coins to melt them and join all the small pieces to create new money, they even used the revaluation of the currency, how is that? The Government took a coin and then stuck a zero next to the 1 and suddenly they converted 1 coin into 10 coins using the same piece. All this eventually led to hyperinflation, tax increases, and economic chaos.

After the First World War, Germany also started printing money to pay for war reparations, this led to hyperinflation and eventually brought Hitler to power. Then in 1918 if you were a millionaire in Germany by the end of 1923 you were completely bankrupt, let me give you an example to understand what hyperinflation looked like in Germany after printing money, imagine it is summer, you are suffocating. You want to go to the beach to have a few beers, and to start instead of ordering 1 beer to drink it and then ordering the second and enjoying it, you order both at once, you know that the second beer is going to get quite hot but still you buy two beers at the same time because when you finish the first one you won't be able to buy the second one, this is hyperinflation. This is the disastrous result of uncontrolled money printing.

The Romans did it, the Chinese did it, the English did it and so did the French and it always ends badly.

Now the United States is doing it, so it is clear that governments never learn from monetary history. Einstein once said, "insanity is doing the same thing over and over and expecting different results", so now that we understand what it means to print money let's talk about the end of the Gold Standard in 1971 under the Breton Woods agreement. This event sped up money printing even further, as the world was trading on the Gold Standard, meaning that other currencies were pegged to the dollar. The dollar was pegged to gold, all at a fixed exchange rate. For every dollar in circulation there had to be an equal amount of gold stored in the reserve. In case some country needed gold it could exchange it for dollars and vice versa. Theoretically in the Gold Standard the Government should not simply print money without increasing its gold reserves, however, in reality the United States printed money even at the time of the Gold Standard. It got to the point where there was a lot of money in print that was not there. backed by gold, then if people began to demand gold in exchange for their US dollars they could not meet the demand.

The next logical step from the US perspective was to end the Gold Standard, which finally happened in 1971. US President Nixon cut the last link between gold and the dollar, meaning that the United States could now print money. easily, as much as I want. Thus, money became a tool in the hands of the government and politicians. Since 1971 the United States has made 3 quantitative expansions and each time the situation worsens more. If printing money is like building a house in the sand, we know that it will eventually collapse, but instead of stopping construction and finding a solid base, we continue building. When problems arise, we simply find some way to prevent the house from collapsing. Therefore, once it starts printing, it is very difficult to stop it because stopping it means tearing down the house and starting over. That is something that most politicians do not want to do during their term. They would be remembered for that. So, everyone is taking the issue to the next administration and the show goes on.

If you want to see the effects of money printing, look at the following factors: from 1913 to 2018 the dollar has lost 95% of its purchasing power. This makes life difficult for those who work for money, for example, the number of food stamps has reached a very high level. In case you don't know, the food stamp is a government support for people who do not earn enough money to live. The middle class is shrinking, the gap between rich and poor is extremely high, the weight and size of the products in the markets are reducing, it seems that it has the same price and the same product, but the weight of the number of packages in the interior is minor, it is very similar to the coin cutout we discussed above, but this time it is happening in products.

When the economy is in a bubble, stock prices and real estate prices go up, everything looks good outside except that average people get poorer and poorer. Look at the interest rates on savings accounts, it's around 1% to 2%, there's a lot of money in circulation, and the banks don't want your money. Now, you can look at this and say that it only happens in the United States and that it does not apply to other countries, but I think this kind of thinking would be too naive because the world economy is more united than ever.

About 70% of world currencies are held in US dollars, with the dollar being the world's reserve currency. You do not have to be an economics professor to understand that if the United States falls, the whole world falls too. Another dangerous thing is that almost all the currencies in the world are fiat currencies which means they are just paper, there is no gold or anything else to back it up and history shows that all fiat currencies eventually go back to their original value which is zero. There is no evidence to show that the same will not happen to the dollar, especially when the dollar has already lost 95% of its value, and now, how long do you think it will take to lose the remaining 5%?

What we are currently experiencing is not a financial crisis but an educational crisis. People do not understand what is happening and this is how governments can get away with printing money. It is not only the United States Government, they also print money other governments. The fact that we do not learn anything about money in school or universities is not a mistake or an accident, it is part of the plan. In the past they did not allow slaves to write or read. Otherwise, the slaves could start demanding their rights as human beings, which happened many years later.

The government is pointing us in a certain direction and that direction is not designed to benefit the average person, it is designed to benefit Wall Street and the ultra-rich. Most of us are recommended to work hard, save money, invest in something long term in the Stock Market, but I tell you the following, you just must think for a moment and compare these tips with the facts that we have discussed previously. And wondering if it makes sense to work hard for money when working harder leads to paying more taxes and the money you earn loses its value as product prices rise, does it make sense to save money when the government prints money? Does it make sense to invest long-term in the Stock Market when the Stock Market is being manipulated and companies take a large part of their profits through fees?

It is time for you to start questioning and investigating all the things you have been told and soon you will realize that none of them work in your favor.

Let's talk now about the present. When a crisis occurs, the people who suffer the most are those on the left side of the money flow quadrant, which are the employees and the self-employed, because these are the people who work for money and will be the first to lose everything. purchasing power and capacity. True wealth is on the right side of the money flow quadrant, people on this side don't work for money, they work for assets like land, real estate, and businesses. Therefore, the recommendation will always be to transition from the left side of the quadrant to the right side where there is true wealth and to do so it is recommended to choose one of the following 4 asset classes: businesses, real estate, commodities, and paper assets like stocks and bonds.

Business is the most difficult asset class to acquire, but also the most profitable. On the other hand, paper assets are the easiest to acquire, but the least profitable and riskiest, so it is not recommended to invest in paper assets, even if you have heard the opposite a thousand times, and that is that the Stock Market It has become a great casino where the winners are always the owners. The best asset of all will always be real estate and I think it would be even better if you choose something you are passionate about.

Let's talk now about the future. To recap what we have discussed so far, let us remember that the past and to this day the Government prints money, which affects people who work for money and save money. We learned that true wealth is on the side right side of the money flow quadrant in the present context. Finally, in this part we will share some tips on transitioning from the left side to the right side of the money flow quadrant.

The first tip is to educate yourself financially, for this there are many books about it, starting with personal finances, through investments and business development, there are also games like monopoly and cashflow, the latter by Robert Kiyosaki, and it is because playing a flow games of Cash is the best way to learn the basics of economics, since when we do something we remember up to 90% of what we learned, then you move on to real life and start applying all this knowledge.

The second tip is to become an entrepreneur. Employment and entrepreneur are two completely different people. Their approach differs a lot. We always hear that you have to study and get a good job in a big company, but we rarely hear studying hard and being an entrepreneur. That's why people don't know each other. Realize that there is another option, they do not even consider it an option, and that is that we are qualified enough to ask for fish but not to fish, that is the basic and main function of schools and universities, you want to do. How you would like to live , definitely the world needs employees to function, it is your choice where you want to be, working class, or the company's owner. In communism, the government must build the houses and provide jobs, but individuals build the economy in capitalism. Unfortunately, most people still live in the communist mindset and expect the government to take care of everything. I insist, the best option by far is to take a risk and become an entrepreneur because the taxes in the law are written in favor of entrepreneurs since they are the ones who are building the economy by creating new jobs, developing real estate and investing. The Government needs entrepreneurs, otherwise, there would be no jobs and the Government could not collect taxes, and I know that for many people becoming an entrepreneur is very risky, they prefer a secure job in a company, but there is no secure job anywhere anymore. Most jobs move to underdeveloped countries or extreme poverty where wages are extremely low, as is India, China, and the Philippines.

Having a job is riskier than becoming an entrepreneur. When you have a job you only have one client, your employer. If they fire you, you will be in serious trouble, but you have many clients if you are an entrepreneur.

Third tip, do not live below your means, expand your means. If you go to a financial planner, they will make you analyze your expenses and ask you to cut your budget, living a life of limitations, invaded by fear and mental shortages. How about we look at the other side of the equation and look for ways to expand our means so that the price of our cravings turns to nothing. Cutting expenses is a passion killer. Do not kill your passion, rather find ways to fuel your passion, always ask yourself how you can afford it.

The fourth tip would be to learn how to use debt and taxes to acquire more assets. Since 1971 money has become debt, when people tell you to get out of debt they say get out of money, of course I am talking about good debt which is debt used to buy assets that puts money in your pocket, We are not talking about passive debt, which is buying or acquiring televisions, cars, vacations, etc.

Fifth tip, don't be afraid of making mistakes and failing, it's just part of the process, just remember how many times you had to fall before you learned to ride a bike successfully. I must clarify that I consider myself a financial expert but I do not have any certification in the area, but I assure you that I earn more money than most of those who do have beautiful titles hanging in their homes or offices, however, to take care of legal aspects, the recommendation is that you look for a specialist in the area of business and investment and in parallel do your own research so that you do not believe and apply everything you hear, remember, you must question thoroughly, this is the only way that in the future yourself You can become an expert in finance and investment walking towards wealth, limiting something else, that the road will be difficult, surrounded by uncertainty, stress and responsibilities, but don't worry, if getting rich isn't your thing out there, there are many small jobs that you can do to earn a living and live poor but honest, although here you have already learned enough fundamentals to understand that you can live a millionaire and honest, and if e These reading this book I welcome you to the roller coaster ride of entrepreneurship.

HOW TO THINK ABOUT MONEY

- the wealth mindset -

"Nothing is sweeter than honey, except money."

Benjamín Franklin

The way you think about money will determine your success or failure in attracting it, because money will only enter your bank account if you discover how to attract it. I do not mean the fantasy of closing your eyes and imagining that money flows like a river towards you. all your bank accounts, that's only part of the strategy, as visualization is extremely important.

However, programming your mind with abundance and eliminating the possible scarcity and poverty files installed in your thoughts will be key to everything financial and economic works in your life. Unfortunately, since we are born, in most cases, we are exposed to bad economic programmers in our environment, possibly our parents are not rich, nor are any relatives, nor do we live in a neighborhood of millionaires, on the other hand we may not have friends either wealthy. All this translates into the comments, customs, philosophies, lifestyles, comments, and ways of reacting and behaving concerning money: poverty and scarcity, or in any case of limitations, and that is fatal. Added to this, we have all the television, radio and tabloid press that distort what it is to be a millionaire. Finally, this storm of misconceptions leaves you stunned and confused not knowing where to start.

Relax, there is a solution, you have supernatural power in your hands, the ability to program your mind and make decisions, that makes you a kind of superhero. You can transform yourself and reinvest in whatever you want.

Now, I am going to share with you a series of comparisons between poor and rich, so that you have clarity of thought regarding how you should think to get rich and richer and richer, and what you should avoid getting away from poverty.

Please keep in mind that when I say millionaire, I mean people who have earned their millions through moral and ethical legal ways, and when I say poor I do not mean to belittle poor people, in fact I have been poor for the most of my life.

Now, your body is like a computer, where your physical body as such is the hardware and the software part would be your mentality, that is, the mentality of a person is the software, therefore, if something is wrong with any part of the Hardware of your computer such as the keyboard or the screen, you can change it easily, but if you have problems with the software it is more complicated, the computer stops working correctly, you would have to reset the machine, update the software, download antivirus, check files, memory, etc. The same goes for humans, if you have a poor person's mentality you cannot be rich, in that case you must update your software to the rich version.

I will begin by explaining the 17 differences presented in the book "*The Secrets of Millionaire Minds*", one of my favorites. I will do it in a very simple way, and then I will add several more on my part to complete 21 differences.

The first difference is that the rich think big and the poor think small. Have you ever gone to the supermarket to buy food and spent several hours in various stores to find the cheapest things and save 50 or 60 cents? if you have done this then you have a poor person mentality, sorry to say that but let me explain, of course you save money, and part of that is also about the get rich game but this changes when it comes to how much you will save in comparison with the time you will spend if you spend an hour to find the cheapest oranges and tomatoes to save 60 cents, in that case the value of your hour is 60 cents. Compared to that, rich people think about the value of their time and constantly think about investing their time in projects and new things they can do so that their hour's value is equal to $ 6,000.00 or $ 60,000.00.

The second difference is that rich people prefer to be paid based on results and poor people demand to be paid based on time. Many times, I hear how people complain that they deserve more salary just because they have been working for the company for 5 years, but in reality things do not work like that, for example if I spend 200 hours writing a poor quality book of course that it doesn't matter how long I've spent doing it, it only matters if the book is good or not. Nobody cares how much time you spend on anything; the real question is if you can deliver something valuable, it is about the result, the effort, not the time spent.

The third difference is that the rich think of obtaining both if two opportunities are presented to them, the poor instead think either the 1 or the other. Poor people feel that it is not enough and that you cannot have everything. The rich think that there is much for everyone and that you can have everything you want, the poor believe in scarcity, and the rich believe in abundance. You want a successful career, a close relationship with your family, how about both? you want to focus on business or have fun and play, how about both? do you want a blonde or brunette girlfriend? Just kidding! The poor always think that they can only get one thing in the best of cases, the poor see the world as a cake and believe that if everyone takes a piece the cake will be over soon. On the other hand, rich people see the world as a 24-hour buffet where once something is finished, they go and replace it at once. For example, money is an important aspect of life and of course happiness is too, and you can have both. Many people have negative feelings about being rich. They think that getting rich makes you a bad person. They think they have to choose between being rich and being nice, so they choose to be nice and stay broke. You have probably heard someone say, "that person changed after getting rich", I believe that money does not change you, money makes you more than you already are, if you are a kind person then money makes you a person rich and kind, if you like helping other people money gives you the option to help more people to a greater extent. On the other hand, if you are an idiot, money will make you more of an idiot, if those bad things after getting rich you were already bad without having money, money only made it obvious what you already were deep down.

Fourth difference, rich people focus on opportunities while poor people focus on obstacles. It is my favorite, every time I come up with a new idea, I share it with people to get feedback, it is very rare to see someone who knows the problems related to the idea, but at the same time sees the opportunities it can provide, almost always I hear poor people constantly talking about obstacles, risks and always focus on problems while rich people focus on opportunities. The poor make decisions based on fear, their minds are constantly searching for what is wrong, what could go wrong in any situation. Their main mindset is what if it does not work? This is how the poor man thinks, and many times it won't work, I'm not saying don't deal with problems, of course handle problems as they arise, but don't allow fear and problems to be your focus. If you focus on opportunities you will have opportunities, it is a simple universal law.

The fifth difference is based on the fact that rich people associate with positive and successful people, poor people associate with negative or unsuccessful people, in short, if you want to fly with the Eagles, don't hang out with the ducks. If your goal is to be rich, study rich people, spend time with rich and successful people, use them as a role model, do what they do, and read what they read. The rich emulate and shorten time, for example, if you want to create a successful YouTube channel, look for successful channels in your field and study what they do, study what type of content they have created, how long their videos last, what kind of style they use, and if you do the same actions, have the same mindset.

You are likely to get terribly similar results. When I give this advice, people get very angry and they say to me "So you want me only to copy other people? Do you want me not to be original? Do you want me only to steal other people's work?" No, I am not saying any of that, what I am saying is that if you are an ordinary guy like me then you have a better chance of being successful modeling successful people and that does not mean that you are not original, for example if you decide to create the summary of a book, suppose it is the same, surely you will find several summaries made by other editors, and it will be the same book but your content will remain unique because you have a particular way of writing and using expression signs, pauses, expressions and guesswork, you have a unique way of explaining things, your cover and presentation will be unique.

Another complaint I hear a lot is that "I don't have rich people around me" so how can you surround yourself with rich and successful people? And you don't have to have them by your side or in front of you, you can simply find successful people and read their books, watch their videos and follow them on social networks, I personally do not have rich friends around me, simply the authors of these kinds of books are rich friends for me, I meet them reading their books, watching their videos and listening to their podcasts.

Let's go with the sixth, rich people know what they want and commit to getting it, the poor only want to be rich and remain in dreams. Imagine you and your friend who are walking around the center of the city and you arrive at a food place and say "Hello, I want to buy a baguette", and most likely the salesman behind the checkout will ask you what kind of baguette friend because there are many types, thousands? the same approach poor people use, when it comes to getting rich they just want to get rich.

They don't know exactly what they want, but now suppose you say "Hi, I want a dark baguette, with sunflower seeds, don't put onion, cucumber or tomato" and guess what, the girl gives you exactly what you asked for, the rich act the same way. The number 1 reason most people do not have what they want is because they do not know what they want. You must know what that real life is like for you and you must have a plan to get there, for example, for me the rich life means having the freedom to work when you want, go where you want, eat what you want, do what you want. For example, I do not like taking public transportation and feeling sweaty, especially if I'm going to an important meeting. When I go to a restaurant I want to be able to open the menu and choose what I want without seeing the price, I want to be able to take my parents on a nice vacation twice a year, I want to be able to help the people around me, I want to be able to get up at 11:00 in the morning, go to the sea when it provokes me on a Tuesday afternoon and drive until I stand looking at the horizon and breathe deeply.

At the same time, the sun's rays hit my face, go to the gym in the middle of the day and come back whenever I feel like it, that's my rich life and I have a plan on how to get there.

Seventh difference, rich people are willing to promote themselves and their value, poor people think negatively about selling and promoting. Let me explain it this way, if you had a cure for some type of disease you should go out and say it without thinking, just knowing that you can help thousands of people maybe millions of people and I assure you that the economic reward will come to you by default, but if you On the contrary, you think meticulously about your economic benefit and avoid disclosing the information by being jealous with your discovery, then you would not be releasing all the potential that this excellent achievement has and you will not be able to exploit it, so if you are not promoting then I am losing the opportunity to change my lifetime. Resentful or reserved promotion is one of the biggest obstacles to success.

People who have problems with sales and promotion are generally bankrupt, how can you generate a great income in your business if you are not willing to let people know that your product or service exists, regardless of the work you do you must be good at sales and promotion. Almost all aspects of our life involve sales, for example when you try to convince your partner to go to a restaurant instead of shopping you are selling, if you try to convince your daughter to study you are selling, in fact fair At this moment I am selling, I am selling you my book. You are paying for it with your time, you are paying with minutes of your life and I am not ashamed to sell my book, I am not ashamed to promote it and ask you to recommend it because I know the ideas these kinds of books can help you change your mindset.

Difference eight, the rich say "I create my life" and the poor believe that life is something that happens to them. If you want to create wealth you must believe that you are the one behind the wheel, the poor travel through life as passengers. The rich always sit behind the wheel, did you ever realize that it is generally poor people who spend a lot of money playing the lottery? they have high hopes that someone will just try to pick their name out of a hat and provide them with money and eventually make them rich, you will also find that poor people justify their situation, they say things like "money is not important while money is not important. happiness and love are important", this type of comparison is not correct. Let me ask you a question, is a leg or an arm important? you are probably saying what a silly question, of course both are important. You are right, both are important in the same way, just like money, just like food and water are important.

The poor always act as victims, I have two cousins who grew up in the same town, went to the same school, had the same teachers. Both had poor parents, today one of them is highly successful. The other is not, the interesting thing is that both They use the same reasons for their current situation, the poor cousin blames the educational system for their failure, on the other hand, my rich cousin used the same reasons to succeed, he says "I knew the school system was bad and my parents were poor and that's why I started to focus and learn new things", I mean, I don't blame the system.

Another reason why the poor are poor is because they complain about everything. When people complain they focus on what is wrong in their life, what you focus on expands, and because of that you will receive more than what is wrong, that's why you do the opposite, focus only on the good and positive things and expand them to get the most benefit from absolutely any situation.

Difference 9, rich people manage their money well and poor people manage their money poorly. Money is just a tool, like your computer or your phone that requires you to learn how to use it, which is why we spend many hours learning how to use the computer, but when it comes to money people ignore that fact, and this is something to lend you. a lot of attention, you must learn about money and become an expert in managing it, it seems crazy to me that people ignore this very basic principle because money is something, we sell our lives for working.

Many people fail in money management because they are not educated. The poor complain about their financial situation but do not want to learn. They say it is difficult and complicated and are not willing to learn the basics of money.

The rich are smarter than the poor simply because they have different money habits being more cautious and more reserved to dominate the administration's money. If you want to manage money and decide to start doing it as soon as you have money it is like an overweight person saying that they will start exercising as soon as they stone 20 kg. It just doesn't work that way, if you don't practice and learn in a little you will never be prepared to receive a lot and for that reason alone a large sum of money will never reach your hand, imagine if your child cannot even maintain and take care of his bicycle, would you buy him a car? of course not, the same logic applies in the universe regarding money, even if you borrow money to live you still need to learn to manage that money, the most important thing is to exercise the muscles of money management so that it becomes a habit, developing the habit first is very important, for example, if your goal is to lift 10 kg and then get to lift 100 kg you must first learn to lift a 1 kg blanket, that blanket is your blanket with which you wrap yourself and so much You have a hard time getting off yourself in the morning and getting out of bed, so you should start with what you have right now.

To start I recommend you create 3 accounts; investment account, game account, education account. Put 10% of the income after taxes in your investment account, it is the account that will create the hen that lays the golden eggs, the intention is to create your own business seeking financial freedom. It is also recommended to put an amount equal 10% in your game account so that you have fun and feel rich and happy, this will take your brain to the ecstasy of always going for more to live well and each time increase your quality of life, and another 10% destined to your financial and business education, always looking for new opportunities and preparing to face situations and take opportunities, always prepared to advance and grow, this is extremely important because today you earn the amount of money that corresponds to the information you have in your head, if you want to earn more money you must put new and more information in your head.

Tenth difference, the rich are bigger than their problems, the poor are smaller than their problems. The secret to success is not trying to avoid problems or learn to handle them, the secret is to grow so big that you are bigger than any problem. It does not matter if you are rich or poor, you are going to face problems. The problem is not the problem, what matters is your size against the problem. The greater the responsibility you can handle, the greater the number of employees you can handle and more. money you can handle. The things we call problems are situations. We decide if we make them a problem, some people make them a problem and others are not even affected by the same situation. For example, someone is fired and spends their entire day depressed while someone else is spending all their free time now to start their own business.

Difference number 11, rich people are excellent recipients, the poor are poor recipients. A poor receiver is a person who cannot receive well, for example, when we receive compliments, compliments, money, gifts and many other things, many of us have problems receiving things, simply with open hands and it is because we are conditioned that way, we grew up hearing things like that is wrong because you have to work hard to have anything in life. The things given away are not valued, that is wrong, you are not doing well, you strengthen the feeling of not being good enough and not feeling good enough to receive things, and that is one of the reasons we are poor recipients. From now on take everything that someone offers you, if someone tells you that you look good, say thank you, even if you feel horrible, that's how it is, just say thank you and receive your compliment.

When I go down the street and I see a coin on the floor I pick it up even though today I am rich, and he declared aloud "I am a money magnet, thank you, thank you, thank you."

Difference number 12, the rich play the money game to win and the poor play the money game not to lose. In sports teams that play strictly defense and no offense have a hard time winning, unfortunately most people play the money game on defense, where their main concern is survival rather than wealth and abundance. The poor want to have enough money to pay the bills, and what you must do is aim high, you must shoot for the stars so that you can at least reach the moon, if your goal is to feel comfortable you will probably never get rich, but if your goal is to get rich you end up extremely comfortable.

Difference number 13, the rich have their money working hard for them while the poor work hard to earn their money. The poor depend on their humor to start producing their money but for the rich they approach this situation differently, they think that it is only mental, they know that they must strive to produce money paying a price to put money to work for them finally, they understand the natural process, but poor people see endless and exhausting work, they only think about finishing their day to rest and repeat the cycle the next day, rich people believe that for their money to work instead of them you must first work hard and they also know that the more they work and produce money, the later all that money will work for them and then rest and work much less, so your first objective should be to become financially free and do it as soon as possible.

The way I see financial freedom is this; It is the ability to live the lifestyle you want without having to work or depend on someone else, and this is achieved when your passive income exceeds your expenses.

Many people cannot differentiate between being rich and being financially free, they think that you must first be rich and then be financially free, but it is not true, financial freedom comes first because it is easier and faster to do, let me ask you a question, is it easier to go up a level on a ladder that has steps? Of course, the ladder of steps is easier because you climb it step after step.

By using this energy we can say that you are becoming financially free, so getting rich is like climbing the ladder and reaching the top. For example, at the beginning of my business adventure I had a house that was costing me to pay the mortgage, after learning basic and simple things about how to manage myself, I simply rented the house and moved to a cheaper apartment, the income from the rent of the house was enough to cover the rent of the apartment and all my expenses plus I could even save some money, and that's exactly what I did.

With that basic idea I started to build my real estate empire, getting properties that would pay me other until I could release them and move on to the next. Focus on the rungs of the ladder first and create enough passive income so that you don't have to work for someone else. Now, once you have stabilized that there are two main sources of passive income, the first is money working for you, this includes investment earnings, financial assets such as stocks, bonds and other assets that appreciate, the second source The main passive income is a business working for you, this implies generating continuous income but here you must be personally involved so that that business flourishes until you can systematize it and place someone in charge as a general manager that you give a good salary and you only have to supervise as president.

Difference number 14, the rich focus on their net worth and the poor focus on their earned income. When it comes to money the common question people ask is how much money you have, and the right question is how much net worth you have, and a small number asks this question of people, the wealthy. Wealth is measured by net worth and it has always been and always will be, to find out your net worth all you have to do is add the value of everything you own, your money, your business, your residence, your belonged in vehicles, stocks, jewelry and then from all this you must subtract everything you owe, what remains would be your net worth. That is your measure of wealth, because one last extreme measure in a difficult situation can turn all of that into money. One thing that I take as a habit is to review my assets every 6 months to set growth goals, remember that what you measure is the only thing that can grow.

Difference number 15, the rich control fear, the poor succumb to fear. Thoughts produce feelings, feelings lead to actions and actions lead to results, for example, if you think of a hamburger, then a feeling of wanting to eat a hamburger is created. You would go out to buy one, which will lead you to increase from weight if you don't control that thought. Thoughts are part of your inner world, being overweight is part of your outer world, action is the bridge between the inner world and the outer world. If there is no action in your thoughts and feelings about getting rich, you are far from getting rich. Many people are reading these kinds of books to get rich but most of them do not take steps to apply what they learned, so it is not about how many books you read, it is about how many books you apply in real life. For example, if I spend all day looking at the girl's photo that I like on Facebook instead of going to talk to her, nothing will happen, probably another guy who if he is determined to take action will keep it.

Fear is what prevents them from taking these measures, doubt and worry are the most common barriers not only to success but also to happiness, and that is one of the biggest differences between the rich and the poor, because the rich are current willing, they even feel fear, even if they feel uncomfortable, the poor on the other hand allow fear to stop them and paralyze them, they do not want to feel uncomfortable, if you are willing to do what needs to be done and you are uncomfortable then you can master the fear, remember that everything is in your mind, our mind is capable of showing us dozens of horrible cases to stop us, our mind is the best horror script writer, so you must train and manage your own mind, that is the most important skill that you must improve, for this I recommend you read a book called "The Power of Now" by Eckhart Tolle and another very powerful book called "Power Without Limits" by Tony Robbins, and to close with a flourish t I highly recommend "The Magic Of Thinking Big" by David Schwartz. The rocks are always willing to ignite that is why they constantly grow and their riches, but the poor think they already know everything and those are the most dangerous words on this planet and for the universe because they condemn you to poverty.

Difference number 16, the rich are good managers of their money while the poor are wasteful and very bad managers. This may seem obvious, but if it were, everyone would be rich and they are not, most are poor, as much as 95% of the world's population, and that is that the principle of being a good administrator lies in making good decisions in each situation that involve money, and that starts with your family budget; food, rent or mortgage, public services, fun and some extras that are luxury such as amazon prime, Netflix, Spotify among others, from there your good or bad administration begins through delayed gratification where again 95% of people fail because They do not have emotional intelligence or mental control, they only think of immediate satisfaction, and all these money leaks are what make you spend more than you earn and that when the month ends you do not understand where the hell your weekly payment money went or biweekly or monthly, you feel tired, exhausted, overwhelmed, dismayed that you have worked so much and that your pay money lasts in your account no more than 5 minutes after paying all the expenses or the famous bills.

To put control in this I recommend a very basic but very effective administrative strategy that consists of taking paper and pencil or for the most modern open an Excel file. On the left side put all your income. On the right side all your expenses, total both and then subtract them to see if you are positive or negative. Still, yes, for it to work you must put absolutely everything, even the coffee you drink in the morning at Starbucks before arriving at your office.

Then you must face the expenses and start eliminating unnecessary things, but calm down, when you manage to stabilize the accounts and start saving you will be able to subscribe to Netflix and amazon prime again, this will be a momentary measure to get ahead.

Difference 17, constantly learning and growing, that's how the rich think, while the poor think they already know everything. This great difference means that the rich invest a lot in education to prepare and learn new things that will take them further and further, specializing in their fields seeking to stand out and dominate their markets, but on the other hand it is difficult for the poor to invest in a market. business or entrepreneurial seminar, in new technologies training or master class on mindset and metal programming, the poor consider that all this is for fools and that it is very boring, and that is why they die poor because they do not invest the largest and most important asset of everyone, themselves and their brain.

Difference 18, the rich admire rich people but the poor envy rich people and that keeps them away from learning and keeps them at a distance from association circles that allows them to keep adding tools and skills learned through emulation. That paradigm creates bad thoughts or negative thoughts for the poor about money and success, and for this I tell you a story about an individual I met in high school who was rich and everyone criticized him because he had a luxury home , luxury cars, luxurious trips and very good clothes, and they all judged them saying that he was a criminal and that he was evil because the rich are like that, and several years later I had the opportunity to talk to that person and I knew that most of his childhood he had spent in poverty, which motivated him to work more and finally he became CEO of a large company.

I tell you that these thoughts will only bring poverty to your life and no benefits. If you keep doing what you are doing and do not introduce positive changes in your life the years will continue to pass. You will continue being poor, because you will get older and stupid instead make you older and wiser.

Difference number 19, the rich know the importance of financial education and understanding the difference between an asset and a liability, the poor do not. Understanding this difference is the most important step to get rich, in short, assets are something that puts money in your pocket and liabilities are something that takes money out of your pocket, for example; if you have a car and you rent it then this is an asset, but if you have a car only for your use then this is a liability when you take money out of your pocket every month for repairs and maintenance in general. Other examples of assets can be rental properties or company stocks, and liabilities are things like the phone you carry and the car you drive.

Rich people focus on increasing their assets while poor people buy liabilities with their income, for example, poor people buy the latest iPhone to be fashionable, but rich people buy Apple shares to generate residual income. Assets are like a tree, you have to take care of it for years until its roots are deep enough to provide shade and then bear fruit, on the other hand, the poor want immediate enjoyment and unfortunately many people want to get rich quickly without learning about money and that's how to build a skyscraper with little or no foundation and that's why people with no financial education can earn tons of money but after a few years lose everything.

Difference 20, The rich learn to understand taxes and accounting, the poor find this very boring. In order to accumulate wealth you must learn to conserve money after earning money, if a rich person earns $ 10,000.00 then they keep everything, but if a poor or middle class person pays a lot of taxes, between 30% and 40%.

You already know that at the beginning there were no taxes and the Government created taxes, however the rich are very financially intelligent and found legal ways not to pay taxes, while the poor and the middle class earn money and can earn big sums but on that money they pay a lot of taxes, practically half of their earned money is given to the government, and the government favors the rich because they have found a way to recirculate money by investing more and more in their businesses, expanding them and generating more and more jobs and consequently generate more income and on that income they must pay more taxes and instead of handing it over to the government what they do is that they further expand their businesses and employ more people and then earn more money and repeat the cycle over and over again because they understand how money works.

Difference number 21, the poor believe in luck and destiny while the rich believe in action. Rivers invent money, create it, and the people who get ahead are not necessarily the most educated. The people who get ahead are the most daring and adventurous. Some people have money but cannot produce more to become millionaires or rich because they cannot see the opportunities, therefore, they cannot take advantage of them due to fear and doubt, most of them sit and wait for the opportunity and what happens it is that it passes through their noses and they are unable to identify them.

Therefore, luck does not exist, money must be created, it must be the product of ingenuity, effort, risk, visualization, desire, passion, goals, dreams, discipline, perseverance, study , courage and learning. The rich can start from scratch in a trade and work to learn and then grow and become independent, they take risks, they prefer that over job security that only offers them a limited salary without aspiration of growth. For this reason, the rich are willing to go through all the stages and positions of a business to learn in detail everything there is to do and become a specialist, the recommendation for young people is to start in a job where they can acquire and learn knowledge that will be useful for the future, such as in the areas of sales, communication, marketing, accounting, leadership, among others, you must choose a job related to your passion or to what you have identified that you want to do the rest of your life And while that company is paying you a salary, what is happening is that it is paying you and training at the same time for your own company, you are earning triple; money, knowledge and skills.

On one occasion, the well-known author Robert Kiyosaki during an interview with a journalist told her that she wanted to become the best-selling author because she realized that she was a great writer and that she should continue with that until she succeeded. Robert recommended that she take a sales course so that she could promote herself, she became defensive and replied that she had a master's degree in English literature and why go to school to learn to be a salesperson if she is already a professional in literature, she told him that of In fact, she hated being a salesperson and that she hated salespeople because all they want is money. Robert told her that he is not the best author or the most literate, but he is the best-selling author in the world because he has known how to promote himself through strategies sales. Due to this fact, all successful and talented people such as doctors, lawyers, dentists, engineers, artists, etc., have achieved it because they have known how to sell themselves, how to promote themselves and how to combine their skills with financial intelligence.

HOW TO INVEST THE MONEY

- take action and move forward -

"The forewarned son stocks up in the summer, but the scoundrel sleeps at harvest time."

King Salomon

We already know where the money comes from, we also know how it works, we even discover some secrets in addition to learning about how to survive and then how to overcome a financial crisis, and now is the time to know some options on how to invest your money to produce every time and more, that is why I want to share with you some of the most practical and quick-start investment forms that exist and that you can find all of them complete in my book "Passive Income". Please, if you want to comment and share some more forms, send them to me described and detailed to my email; networkmarketingaw@gmail.com.

Let's start:

1 / Videos & Photographs

Audiovisual content is an important source of income today because everything moves through social networks, people around the world are more aware of news, fashion, events, and entertainment than anything else; the news and magazine channels have been digitized, and there are also more powerful sources even now such as TWITTER, INSTAGRAM, FACEBOOK, and YouTube, and the invasion happens through your eyes the average person loses more than 10 hours a week in on social networks because they get caught by entertaining videos or attractive photos one after another. They can't stop watching them, and this can help you generate passive income. You can create your account in any of these media and constantly upload content to increase your followers to reach the point of starting to capitalize.

You can also record videos from your phone about news, happenings, daily life, events, demonstrations, protests, festivals and political conferences, press conferences, conventions and shows and sell it to companies related to these sources of information, you can professionalize this occupation and buy equipment quality to improve your content and also have a better edition.

But if you want this to be your passive job, you can also attend public events such as protests, demonstrations and festivals, record videos, and sell them to the media and online press.

You can also create a Blog to upload the content there and promote your blog to the interested media so that they have immediate access to your videos and photos, and they can offer to buy you the information to have exclusivity.

And there's another way: sell your photos and videos on web pages that are dedicated to selling this type of material to millions of marketers worldwide who need content to create their designs or advertising campaigns, and I leave you some pages here;

-PEXELS

-ISTOCKPHOTO

-SHUTTERSTOCK

-CLIPSTOCK

-PIXABAY

2/ AIRBnB

The applications (APPs) came to globalize businesses and make everyone's life more comfortable and more straightforward, and to give us more possibilities or options to generate income, and that is the case of AIRBNB that allows you to upload properties without a greater protocol to put them in rent, but wait, I know you think that you don't have several houses out there available and don't know what to do with them (hehehehehe!), you can also through AIRBNB rent a room in your house, or you can build in your property an additional space or annex for this purpose with independent access.

I tell you that on one occasion I was planning to go on a trip to the beach (I love the beach) and I was looking for a house on AIRBNB (we would go a large group). I found for rent a couple of "hammocks" known elsewhere as "*chinchorros*", these were at the back of a house that had an exit to the sea, it also had a beautiful view, and they were perfect for a romantic night or a spectacular sunset looking at the horizon, so I called my wife to tell her, and when I came back to show them, and at They had booked (incredible), AIRBNB represents a tough blow to the hotel industry in many countries, including the United States, even in some areas it's forbidden to rent your property through AIRBNB.

AIRBNB is an excellent option to generate a residual or passive income that practically does not require much effort, just upload the promotional photos on the website, review and sign the conditions agreement, keep the space clean, and attractive to guests, and maintain the place, so it doesn't deteriorate, and that's easier than working at a McDonald's. The best thing is that you don't have to commit to a long-term rental so that you can stop this activity at any time.

3/ Create a Personal Website – Blog

You can create a web page from scratch, it's simple, and you start from the most basic by shaping your page. You should think of an initial topic, and begin to shape it, upload content, photos, images, videos, and copywriting, and once you start to get known, and get organic traffic, you can begin connecting or linking a variety of things/tools to your website to monetize it, such as advertising, affiliate LINKs either of products, services or courses related to your topics. Still, you can also sell your products, either your creation, and resale of some brands that you recommend from experience that you are demonstrating on the subject.

This can become a constant source of passive income, so much so that many, if not most, or almost all or all Digital Marketing specialists have pages of this type.

Here the advantage is free imagination because you can practically create a website of absolutely anything you can think of because there's something very safe, human diversity is impressive, and here you can unleash your imagination and creativity. The best of all is that you will not have anyone controlling you or respecting any rule, the page is yours, and you control and command it, it's something independent, here your success is in your hands, and you can create your brand and your style, and That is something very sold today, people love that which is represented by someone, that which is presented by its creator, by someone normal, someone like you and me who was able to build something and achieve success, That, the human is much sought after today, and the public applauds creativity.

4/ Dropshipping

This is one of the methods of sale by internet or electronic commerce most used nowadays, since it basically consists of creating a web page to sell products that you don't manufacture or produce and that you don't keep in stock either, so it consists of a Triangulation of retail product sales shipments where the retailer does not store the goods in his inventory, but takes and passes the order (and shipping details) to the wholesaler or manufacturer, who dispatches the products directly to the end customer or consumer

Triangulation can be on a product or service order and occurs when a retailer, who typically sells in small quantities to the general public, takes the order for one or more units of the product or service and passes all this detail on automatic to the manufacturer or wholesaler who supplies or dispatches from his establishment or warehouse directly to the buyer.

The shipment can be in "masked package," which means that it does not include the sender, so as not to identify the retailer that it's not the source of dispatch. In some cases, the address or identification of both is placed, or failing that the retailer receives the appointment of "distributor or authorized service center."

The retailer, that is, you, receives a commission or percentage on each sale made, taking advantage of the margin between the wholesale and retail prices. Said price will always be previously fixed in a "Triangulation Contract" on the conditions of sale.

Dropshipping is one of the most profitable ways to generate more income.

This is a method that can be systematized and left on autopilot since everything can be synchronized from your website, and I leave below a list of platforms where you can start your first dropshipping business;

-Volusion

-Shopify

-Squarespace Online Store

-WixStore

-Square Online Store

-BigCommerce

-WordPress Ecommerce

-WooCommerce

5/ Stock Exchange

Investing in shares of the stock market is one of the best types of passive or residual income that can exist. The only downside is that you will need to have investment capital.

I also recommend you run away from all Network Marketing or MLM companies that may offer you to develop or invest in the stock market through these schemes because, in reality, this market does not work that way. You will realize that in reality what they offer you is a study system to prepare or teach to invest and it happens that in most cases (99%) who teaches you isn't an expert and is very far from Wall Street, simply It's someone who registered a couple of months before you but simply speaks well and believes what he says (hehehehehehe!), so the recommendation is that you look for a broker, and in most banks you will find this service, in fact there are banks specialized in this subject and where you put the money and they play with it, and literally they play with it, since the world of the stock market is a kind of casino where you enter with a bet and you can win or lose and this can happen very quickly, that is, you can earn a lot of money in a matter of seconds or minutes and in other cases in a few hours, but the same way you can lose everything, and that's what these are about, these markets are aggressive in most cases and it's because they depend on a lot of factors that can be very difficult to define and that is why you have to look for specialists who know more about placements and short and long-term behavior, therefore based on this it's always better to start on the stock market with stable stocks, which don't generate many profits or dividends but are safer, have moderate but more stable growths, and these stocks are those that come from government agencies, funds government, army, insurance, health, etc., and apart from these markets we have Gold.

I recommend you study hard, take stock and placement courses, finance, and economics courses so that you can better understand the terminology and terms and to be able to understand your broker and demand or discuss some decisions until maybe one day you feel ready to take control.

I leave you some of the most recognized brokerage houses in the United States, of which almost all can be contacted online and start investing without having to be in the United States;

-TD Ameritrade
-Etrade
-OptionHouse
-TradeKing
-Scottrade

6/ Sell Websites And Online Stores

Here is a detail, you must know how to program, but if you don't know you can learn, so you could create passive income by selling websites and online stores.

This way of generating passive income requires a little more effort since you must have the prior technical knowledge or acquire it through courses and practice. Also, after creating your websites and/or virtual stores you must check that it works, that is, practically the game is to sell an operating business and billing, which takes time; however, many people are willing to pay for those virtual companies that behave like assets because once they begin to practically bill the traffic they keep up with advertising or sales funnels that take people to the website. There the process is automated, of course you have previously programmed it that way.

Here it's a matter of finding a winning product to put it in front of a niche and start billing.

Also, instead of selling the website or the virtual store you can rent or rent it and earn a percentage of the sales that are being made. Thus, you earn less but you get a monthly income, of course the first case would be a direct sale and a single profit for each site or website sold, and here in this 2nd modality your client may not have the capital to buy the website because they only have or have capital to invest in the merchandise they must buy to cover sales. I would also like to try the store and profitability before moving on to the purchasing step.

And if you already have a site like this or are thinking about starting to create it, here is a platform that allows you to put it up for sale, because I'm sure you were wondering: And after creating the site and putting it into operation, who the hell I sell it to him? And here comes the answer;

Exchange Marketplace, the Shopify exchange market.

7/ eBooks

Many people love to write but have never dedicated themselves to it because they think that becoming a famous writer is a very complicated matter, and perhaps that was many years ago. Still, today the internet once again broke that paradigm. Because you can write a book about absolutely what you can think of without having to print it and go through hundreds of publishers who have to read your book and wait weeks for a queue of hundreds of books to be evaluated so that in the end they tell you not to. they are interested in your book, because today isn't a problem. You can let your imagination run wild, write an eBook on the topic of your preference, choose something that you are passionate about so you can flow, and edit it yourself, next step, publish it on your social networks, publish it through FaceBook or Instagram, or Better yet, sign up for the Amazon Kindle program and have access to millions of readers eager to find literary works on various subjects by unknown authors, as well as You.

So, if you like to write, go ahead, go ahead, it's easy, and there are infinite endless niches because there's something for everyone. And I'm going to tell you something, there are thousands of new writers sitting in front of a LapTop writing at home, in the parks, on the subway, on the beach or anywhere making money through this very lucrative method, which It's a million-dollar industry. It's super accessible since it's just writing your book that does not have to be a 500-page literary work, it can merely be a good writing with good content of 30 pages, but come here, in Amazon for example enters a market of 150 million subscribers in 72 hours maximum after being approved by the review team, and uploading that manuscript can take 10 minutes after having it finished along with the cover.

Oh, by the way, this is an eBook, I like to write, when I start, I feel like I can't stop and the ideas flow one after another, and if it doesn't work to monetize I wouldn't, I would look for something else to put my time and make money passive.

And there's something extraordinary, if you write an eBook and see that it's having a good reception, you can translate it into any language for just about $ 25 (We are talking about 35 pages) on service platforms like the ones we already saw (example: Fiverr), Imagine the reach that you can have through the internet and on platforms with as much breadth and traffic as Amazon, Aliexpress, eBay, Wish, among others.

8/ Create an APP

It could be said, literally, that today the world is dominated and controlled through APPs, AH! ... wait! You don't believe me? So, look at your smartphone, by the way, guess why they call it that? Smartphone!!! Here is the answer; because it's full of applications that allow you to use your phone for pathetically anything, this is impressive. Let's see, there are applications for; exercise, measure your weight, turn your phone into a magnifying glass, GPS, compasses, calculators, personal income and expenditure management, play, access to all banks, Forex, food deliveries, package deliveries, restaurants, Astronomy, channels from movies and tv series, finance, video editing, music, translators to all languages, travel agencies, tourism, flashlights, social networks, economics, news, radio stations, Ecommerce, chats, videoconferences, calendar, creation and design, and anything that goes through your head, bone, this is an invitation to put your imagination to fly.

I'm going with a statistic; Every day around 5,000 applications are created, of which 90% of them die in the initial phase of exposure to the public, that is, in their period of testing and acceptance, but yes, if you create one that is welcomed in the market, you get rich in a matter of months.

What do you have to do to create an application?

The first thing is to sit down and think about some social problem, something that has to do with the population, and find a practical solution through a simple application that everyone can download to their phones with just a click, and then view it. and start capitalizing.

You must prepare in programming if you want to develop it yourself, or failing that, hire a programming company to help you with the development of it, yes, make sure you sign confidentiality contracts. For that you need a lawyer to I can protect your rights of "Intellectual Property" because otherwise, I assure you, no, I swear, it's more I promise you, they will steal the idea. They will develop it for them to become millionaires.

So here what matters is the creative detail and putting action into the development of the system because we are facing one of the most powerful sources of passive or residual income in recent times, so much so that practically, if your business does not have an APP you are insignificant to the commercial world, what's more, you are harmless, they don't pose any threat, it could be said that you don't exist, at that level we are talking, and it's that I can assure that the entire world or 95% of the civilized planet that we know today will be managed or controlled through applications for the simple reason that almost 95% have access to a Smartphone with internet and consequently what you put on those cell phones it will translate into being in the hands of all the people who have one at a single click, and that is a winning idea that today is already a reality that every day is more potentiated, has even transformed the reality of many spaces physicists and the way of working and earning money for many people.

And now let's talk about some applications that today make the lives of thousands more comfortable and have made their owners super millionaires:

Amazon, eCommerce system where you can buy almost anything, and just like this application, there are other similar ones; eBay, OfferUp, OLX, Alibaba, AliExpress, among others.

UBER, an urban transport system that replaced 95% traditional taxis, as well as; LYFT, CABIFY, and DIDI, among others.

TURO, allows you to rent your car while you aren't using it.

AIR B&B allows you to rent a house, property, or a room.

DoorDash, delivery of restaurant meals at home, as well as; UBEReat and Postmate among the popular.

AMAZON Flex, to deliver packages at home from the Amazon company.

PayPal, for electronic money transfer.

WhatsApp, chat for communications, as well as Telegram, WeChat, Line, and MeetMe as the best known.

Instagram, social network like Facebook, Snapchat, Twitter, Tik Tok, and LinkedIn with the most traffic.

And the invitation is to create yours because this is a passive income.

9/ Funnels

This marketing strategy was super complicated to develop a long time ago, you had to know a lot about programming, creating and designing web pages and integrating tools, and this can be very overwhelming and overwhelming for those of us who aren't so technological, however, today that isn't like that, Because many companies have developed very intuitive software for creating funnels that anyone without programming knowledge, even a child, can do it because it's practically like putting together a puzzle. These systems are full of tutorials that explain step by step everything there's. What to do to build the funnel?

But what is a funnel, and what can we do with it?

A Funnel is a digital marketing tool that allows you to advertise a product or service through the internet, and consists of an advertisement launched through a post or video through social networks or search engines, and they are also added as links in web pages of Blogs, news, companies, and once the interested party is exposed to advertising and clicks, the funnel system is activated since it goes to a page called Capture Page where generally the client leaves his data, almost always name, surname and email and perhaps his telephone number, and immediately goes to a second page where he is shown a little more information presenting the product and making an offer, whose offer always is improved on another page making it increasingly irresistible to complete the sale, and if by chance the client does not buy and tries to leave the page, a message called PopUp appears, indicating that they expect there to be an even better offer, with the intention of lowering the price a little more or offering some additional service product in half the price or increasing the discount, and if by chance the sale isn't completed then that customer will be chased through your email for days, in some extreme cases up to 3 months of daily mail or intermediaries presented and remembering the product or service, almost always offering some things for free, perhaps an eBook, on other occasions a free course or a sample, all this to continue attracting the customer, And last. Still, not least, the most sophisticated will chase you through social networks for any web page you visit during the next 30 days this is impressive, one of the most used and powerful marketing strategies in recent times.

And your friend can use this tool in several ways, leaving you here 2 options;

1/ Build a funnel to capture leads (Prospects), and I'll give you an example; Observe in your community some clinics or perhaps some medical centers, aesthetic clinics, Spas or GYM, create a funnel to promote any of these businesses and collect data from those interested, and when you have optimized the funnel and are generating a good amount of daily leads see and offer the funnel to the owners of these businesses as an advertising tool and attract potential customers, and you know what? Do you know how much you can charge? grab your seat, because you can be charging for each of these funnels about $ 1000 to $ 2500 per month, and this is good news because right now I have 3 funnels of this type for which I am charging $ 1500 for each one. I take build each of them around 5 days, and to get the same residual buying real estate product you would have to buy a property of at least $ 150,000.00 for the cheapest.

2/ You can look for a product, analyze it, do a market study, maybe do some reviews on Amazon, eBay and Google to determine a product that is highly received and in demand, and yes, build a sales funnel, which was the origin reason for this marketing tool.

I leave you here the most popular and best platforms for the construction of funnels:

-Clickfunnel
-Sumo
-HubSpot
-Smartfunnel
-Wishpond
-Builderall

Funnels behave like passive systems, however, they tend to stop giving results after several months, since people get bored of seeing the same thing and it's long production periods of up to 6 months of results where you only sit to receive the money in your account.

10/ Create a YouTube Channel

Google bought Youtube, and since then there has been an incredibly exponential growth in the display of content in video format; there were even many people who started earning reasonable amounts of money overnight, and others became millionaires. Although today It's not so easy, the opportunity is still present, and new emerging YouTubers always appear.

And I know! You would love to become a YouTuber, become a millionaire by uploading videos to the network, videos without much sense but entertaining, just enough that they have an audience and that can be any niche, as strange as it may seem, you can become a YouTuber by uploading videos of your tattoos every time you get one, or black humor jokes, or just bad jokes, but it can also be about jokes, improvised songs, or also deceiving people by uploading videos revealing magic secrets and hidden strategies to make money online that nobody wants you to discover.

Still, a Youtuber comes and is showing it to you with more than 500 thousand views. If you check well, you find hundreds of other YouTubers in different languages revealing the same secrets and magic formulas (hehehehehe!), but guess what? IT WORKS!

And if it's true that there's more and more competition on YouTube, it's also true that it's the second content search engine on the Internet after Google. It's expected that in a concise time, it will become the first, and that translates into a very high potential. economic, and that this tool is in a second stage of growth, so look for your surfboard and ride the wave.

This method will hardly make you free for life, but surely you can generate an interesting residual, and it can also be a lot of fun, so if you have charisma, don't waste it because the cameras are waiting for you and YouTube wants to pay for it.

Surely you know or have heard of a millionaire Youtuber, however, they aren't the majority they are very few, perhaps many earn a few thousand dollars, which is great, and here is the payment relationship that applies YouTube that will depend on the content, since it varies between humor, children, technology, politics, gossip, etc.

We are talking about an interval of $ 3 to $ 5 per 1000 views.

Being the best paid at the moment, the contents related to Forex, Health video games and curiosities.

Let's get accounts!

You have a channel of 100,000 subscribers, which will probably take 1-2 years to build.

You upload one video per week that gets 50,000 views and YouTube pays you the minimum of $ 3 depending on your content. We would be talking about $ 150 a month for that video, and if you upload 4 videos a month with that average of views we would be talking about $ 600 per month, but residual.

However, apart from the money you can receive directly from YouTube, you can also monetize your channel by receiving sponsorship from companies that make toys, or diapers, or children's clothing, or energy drinks, or tools, wow! video game developers, travel agencies, and for you to count.

I recommend that you start this project as soon as possible because you can build it and it will take several months to grow, but I assure you that you are going to have fun.

We can mention as a last thing that, if YouTube simply causes you to close your channel and it closes and that's it, so be very careful to avoid making a mistake uploading inappropriate content because YouTube does not mess with games.

11/ Audiobooks

I love it, I love it, I love this way of generating money, and I love it so much because it's based on giving added value, creating something and monetizing it, but when I say create, I mean that you should let your imagination run wild, your ability creative, innovative, discover your muse and take advantage of something that you master, some knowledge, some special skill on which you can generate content, write a manuscript and prepare it to be able to record it in audiobook format and start earning money for royalties.

I confess to you that I have not yet dabbled directly with audiobooks. Still, I am already doing the pertinent research to bring all my eBooks to this type of edition since it's very profitable, as much as audiobooks, in fact there's a huge niche of people who prefer 1000 times listening to an audiobook than sitting down to read a book, for the simple reason that in today's hectic and troubled world people who have normal jobs are increasingly flooded with working hours and go from full time to part-time. time and after leaving that part-time they go another (hehehehehehe!), you will say that I exaggerate. Still, many people in the big metropolises work up to 16 hours a day and that is incredible, because if you put the time of transfer to the workplace, the time to get ready and eat, you have maybe 3 hours left and they use them to sleep, I don't think they use them to read, but guess what? While driving to your job site or on the subway, or even on the job site, you can wear headphones and Voilà!! There they begin to listen to an audiobook, and most likely it's an audiobook on personal finances, investments, how to make money from home, how to generate passive income, etc., precisely to see if they find a way out of their rat career and begin to decrease hours of those part-times that are killing them.

I leave you here some platforms where to expose your audiobooks to monetize them;

-Audible

-Audioteka

-Audiolibros

-Audiobooks

-Ivoxx

-Moon Reader

-iTunes

Now, to create your audiobooks I recommend these two platforms;

-AX

-eSpeak

Finally, this is a great and very elegant way to generate passive income, literally royalties for intellectual property on your audio-recorded works. While others listen and delight you sit down to see how the money enters your account, yes, this will work for you if you create quality content that is interesting and well-crafted.

12/ *jingles* or Audio Tracks

This is another elegant way to generate royalties because it consists of creating your audio tracks where you will have their intellectual property. Here again you must look for your muse, your creative capacity, your genius, and take all your talent and monetize it, of course It's that this source of income isn't so easy to create, it's more specialized, and I leave it to unknown artists who can make a lot of money through this medium.

So, if you know how to play a musical instrument you can create some of your original audio tracks, or you can also search for songs that are playing a lot, the most popular ones and you can create or play music from your instrument; piano, organ. Keyboard, flute, guitar, saxophone, clarinet, trumpet, accordion, violin (this is one of the favorites for audio listeners) and then mount it on one of the platforms that work for this, which I leave you here;

-Audio Socket

-Sound Cloud

-Song Freedom

Hey, come here! you don't have to be a dedicated musician either, I have several friends who are sound engineers and create music tracks from computers. These melodies are also highly sought after by young people, especially by the Millennial generation who love techno music, electronics etc. artificially created.

13/ Coaching

Coaching isn't easy, you must be prepared in some specific area, and you must be good if you intend to make money with this method, you must also have patience because you must make a name accompanied by a good reputation in growth that will be what in the end will bring you clientele. Please, don't go into this field if you don't have studies, preparation and/or experience, because you are going to look very bad. Not only that but you will lose time and money others who seek to grow in some area, whether personal or business, that is, don't become one more charlatan of those who abound today in social networks saying that they know a lot about something and know absolutely nothing, because today almost anyone with a few followers already believes in coaching (hehehehehe!).

Another thing to consider in this profession is that it has a difficult scale, since you must be very creative to be able to take this method to a group system that allows you to monetize massively, since most coaching end up working with a few clients already.

that they don't personalize the accompaniment because each case is particular. In that case you must be good but outstanding to be able to charge high rates and be profitable for you. And the fact is that most of your clients are going to want a 1 to 1 face-to-face accompaniment.

Now if you sit down to elaborate a good strategic plan that you can digitize and create a group format, then you hit the nail on the head.

Now, once the whole system is assembled, I assure you that it will be very gratifying to see how you help other people to earn a lot of money, arranging their business, relationships and personal affairs, and at the same time earn money for that, we can say that it's a profession full of purpose.

Here the cornerstone is really to lead your clients to achieve measurable results, and that will depend on all the others, because with one or a group happy with their goals achieved, the rain of clients will arrive eager for you to empty all your wisdom and guidance on them.

To promote this project, you must start by establishing a digital marketing strategy through social networks such as FaceBook, Instagram and Youtube as the main ones, as well as a Blog where prospects can interact and to drive interested traffic in your services. It does not have to be something so elaborate, on top of that what counts is that it's valuable content, that would be the honey for your ants.

Here the groups must be reduced so that you can provide a good experience, and that leads you to demand and prepare yourself more and more, but you can charge a good figure if you demonstrate your capabilities, which will help you earn good income in the medium term.

Something positive and interesting is that places like the United States are very fashionable. The topic of coaching is very popular with figures such as Tony Robbins (Personal Growth), Robert Kiyosaki (Investments and Real Estate) and Grant Cardone (Business and Sales), which has promoted the concept worldwide, with more and more coaching figures appearing and many countries in Latin

America mainly, as well as in Spain and the United Kingdom.

If you are good you will have practically no competition, on the other hand, the risk is almost nil since the investment is meager, and from the point where you have developed your training or coaching program, all you have to do is wait for the prospects while you are advertising to expand and make yourself known, taking advantage of radio programs, community aid, free advice, in the church of your community, social clubs, charity clubs, etc.

14/ Rent out your Car

Here is a simple one, rent your car, and I am going to give you several safe ideas;

UBER, you can rent your vehicle to drivers or drivers to use your vehicle while you aren't using it, for example, when you are at work, at nights when you sleep and on weekends that you will not leave home. Now if you have investment capital then you can buy multiple cars and do the same full time for these drivers. You could be charging an average of $ 50 per day for each standard vehicle, and thus build a systematized business with little supervision and producing passive income, that then at the end of the useful life of the car you can sell it and get capital to buy a new one and keep renewing and expanding your fleet and at the same time increasing your income flow.

HYRECAR, this application allows you to rent your vehicle but in a safer way even than the previous one because everything is managed through an already created system. You only incorporate the cars to the same where they are monitored, and the same application keeps your vehicles available for different drivers that enter the app looking for cars to work, which in turn can be used to operate in various applications such as Instacart, UBEReats, Postmate, Doordash and AmazonFlex. Here the idea is also to create a fleet of vehicles to increase the flow of income more and more.

TURO, this application is very practical because it allows you to systematically and safer the initial idea of renting your vehicle to do UBER, however, in this case the concept changes because here you make your vehicle available while you aren't using it (when you are at work, weekends or at night), and when a TURO user needs a car, then he turns on his application where the closest available vehicles will appear, then simply goes to the car where he takes it and uses it to do so. you want, go to another place, supermarket, the beach, etc., with the condition of returning it in the maximum time limit established by the owner, in other words, You!

In all these cases you already know that the initial idea is to make extra money by renting your vehicle. The second idea is to make this a business by acquiring several cars to create a fleet and generate a greater volume of income, which will require a little more effort, basically administrative and supervisory, of course. At the same time, you build a structure that allows you to hire a person to be in charge of maintenance and to review the fleet daily and the different operational details that come with having a fleet of vehicles that require oil change and filter, tires, fluids, cleaning, etc.

15/ Index Funds

This is a good way to generate passive income, probably one of the best, or perhaps the best of all because you put your money in and that's it! done, wait, unlike TRADING where you must buy and sell shares daily, which isn't residual money at all because each operation depends on you. Incidentally, it's a daily dedication because your profit lies in the profit of each sale positive earned, here you don't need to do anything, you just leave your money working for you. You just leave the money there and forget about their movements, no matter if stocks go up or down.

Here the investment is made in the market in general, not in a specific company, and this favors you enormously because you don't have to worry about details such as choosing specific investments, balancing your portfolio or knowing when to sell or buy, because your investment portfolio will be operating on autopilot.

The great advantage here is that the operating expenses are minimal because the services of research analysts aren't needed and you must regularly pay a broker or stock analyst to select your investments.

This is a very good choice if you have your thoughts in the long term, of course the utility isn't overwhelming, the percentages of profit are usually low but very safe, and the more money you put to work for you in this scheme the more the money will be what will you get in return.

We are talking about an average of 5% for the lowest shares and 15% for the highest, where you can enter with about $ 1000 but with no subsequent investment time, which turns out to be very easy because what you need is capital investment, being this always my option when investing in the stock market. The one that I recommend, in fact it's here where I recommend to go putting all the money of utility obtained from other businesses.

16/ Peer To Peer Loans

Now, this straightforward form brings with it details that you must legally handle to insure your money, you have to analyze the risks very carefully in each particular case, that is, with each person or client, and the recommendation is that the money you are going to use to start this business model it's not a capital that you need immediately or in the short term.

The direct person-to-person loan is also managed for small businesses, in both cases it will almost always be when neither of these two figures qualifies for a traditional or regular loan at a bank.

I must make several recommendations, and the first of them is to thoroughly investigate the profiles of the clients to whom you intend to lend the money, you should also distribute the loans among several people to minimize the risks before an unscrupulous potential client who refuses to pay or widely delay the installment periods and total principal of the loan. On the other hand, I also recommend consulting with an attorney and/or accountant to write a basic and simple but legal document that supports you and commits the client to executing and honoring the loan, this will also help you not to incur any irregularity before the law that can later be used against you, or in any case and the main reason is for any client who refuses to pay.

Finally, definitively this isn't my best option and the one I recommend the most, in fact I don't like it very much. However, I apply it today after many bitter experiences so that it can be a real headache, remember that these Clients did not qualify for a traditional loan at a bank where they could have obtained a much better interest. Yet, they came to you who is probably handling an interest rate of double or triple or sometimes 4 and 5 times more than a bank, obviously Because you don't manage the large funds and capital that a financial institution manages.

Ah, of course, you need investment capital.

17/ Real Estate (REIT)

The expression REIT comes from the English "Real Estate Investment Trust", which is understood as Reliable Investments in Real Estate, and this is the absolute best alternative to invest in the real estate sector passively.

This Alternative consists of not looking for properties on their own, which can take a long time to investigate not only in the legal part of the property but also in its structural and maintenance conditions, since the memory of the owners or sellers often hide damage behind SheetRock, putty and paint, such as broken pipes and termites, among other things. At the same time, here we avoid all this and go to a mutual fund for real estate projects.

We are talking about huge entities that are generally listed on the stock exchange and whose main objective is that small and medium investors can participate in large real estate projects that would otherwise be impossible to access because they would be millions and millions of dollars in most of the cases.

You can work these funds one at a time, that is, you choose one, you put your money there and that would be it, of course you need advice for this. My recommendation is to find a broker that can support this and support you in the operation with their experience, but here security is very, very high since these projects have been evaluated by a team of experts from all points of view, they have projections of 10 years, perhaps 20 years and sometimes up to 30 years in the future with analyzes of all kinds, Therefore, when it has been decided to start the project, its profitability is more than assured, which provides many benefits and a lot of liquidity, making this option a very attractive and better alternative than traditional investment in real estate.

Something very practical is that you don't get tied up, in almost all cases you can sell your fund whenever you want and the value can increase very quickly in a short time. It's because professionals manage them with a lot of experience who know exactly what they do and how to make that money yield, so you only have to get good advice from your broker to study the benefits of the fund and the exit options and then put your investment and see how it grows.

18/ Network Marketing

"Network Marketing emerges today as the most powerful distribution method and the most attractive business model in the new economy".

- From the book The New Professionals by Doctor Charles King, Doctor of Business Administration from Harvard University, and Professor of Marketing at the University of Illinois, Chicago.

Yes, as you are reading it, if you want to build an empire online, and become a billionaire and even a billionaire, Network Marketing is the best option, but not only that, it's the most powerful for the simple reason that you can start with practically nothing. investment and have access to a huge company that operates in many countries and markets who are responsible for absolutely everything; production, guarantees, storage, returns, dispatches, call center, taxes, legality, education, incentive trips and infrastructure. We are talking about a global business where you can earn in various currencies and travel the world knowing cultures and developing leadership and influence, and really impact lives. If this catches your attention then you are in the right place, because these experiences can also be highly rewarding.

But I'm not the one saying it, all these books say it;

"The Business Of The 21St Century"
Robert Kiyosak

"How to Build a Multi-Level Money Machine: The Science of Network Marketing"
Randy Gage

"The WAVE 4 Way to Building Your Downline"
Richard Poe

"My Business of People, 20 Years Later"
Luke Mills

"Go Pro - 7 Steps to Becoming a Network Marketing Professional"
Eric Worre

"Your First Year in Network Marketing: Overcome Your Fears, Experience Success, and Achieve Your Dreams!"
Mark Yarnell

And I can name many more where they will affirm that this business model will take over the world economy in the coming years, since any human being willing to excel through training will be able to create their own independent business that will function as a kind of franchise.

But here I clarify a little more the panorama.

What is Network Marketing?

Network Marketing is defined as how the manufacturer introduces his products in the market in the form of "Business Opportunity ".

Network Marketing is a form of distribution of products and services, directly from the manufacturer to the final consumer, without intermediaries, facilitating through personal consumption and by recommendations to others, generating continuous profits.

What are the reasons that make us decide to be a Networker?

Along the way we have met many lawyers, doctors, managers, architects, small business owners, who abandon "success" and don't look back. Thousands of people of all kinds who recover dreams and illusions, all have joined to the ranks of the new professionals.

Many of them have decided to embrace an industry that they once laughed at, mocked, and vowed never to make contact with.

But what exactly is Network Marketing?

It's the low-cost industry that invites you to develop your own business and obtain potentially high income working from home and on your own schedule.

You get immediate income through the sale (which today you can do 100% online) and significant residual income by reaching products and services directly to consumers and inviting other people to do the same.

Known in the past as multilevel marketing and historically despised for having been considered a pyramid scheme for unsuspecting and manipulative people, it emerges today as the most powerful distribution method, and the most attractive business model of the new economy, today you can get it under the names of Social Commerce and Social Marketing.

I leave you here the list of the first 10 and the most powerful:

You can see that AMWAY doubles the profit of its closest competitor and the 2nd in the list, that is to say, really, it has no competition, therefore, if you are going to start in this business model because enter with any other if you can enter with the first, number 1.

However, maybe you like a particular line of products, perhaps you identify with a market; diet, makeup, health, energizers, vegans, organic, essential oils, etc. You just must be clear that here it will require a lot of work, focus, dedication and hours, but you can do it in your free time spaces, you can see it as part-time, and build something giant in a matter of 3 to 5 years.

I wish you success in your adventure, but it excites me to know that I am not the only one who resists being a slave to the system and burning the best years of his life at the mercy of a job, with a schedule and a boss who end up getting rich, and you further and further from your dreams. Entrepreneurship is the way!

WAYS TO SAVE MONEY

- the seed of wealth is savings -

"An ounce of action is worth more than tons of preaching".

Mahatma Gandhi

Let's review 15 ways to save money.

How to save on insurance. As much as possible, if it can be done, you must seize every opportunity for you to save on insurance.

Here are some tips you can follow.

Your home insurance:

- If you think about it, you can actually save up to several hundred dollars if you buy insurance from a low-price but licensed insurer. Compare prices of the insurance departments in your state and get the lowest price but most practical company.

- Negotiate a lower selling price with a broker who works for you and not as the mediator to the seller. There may be a conflict of interest if there are too many people involved. So negotiate with just the broker.

Your life insurance:

- If you prefer just insurance protection, and not a savings and investment life policy, you can just buy term life insurance.

- If you would like to purchase whole life insurance, then hold on to one up to 15 years. If you cancel these policies after only two years of having them in your name it will mean double the insurance costs.

- Check the public library about life insurance in your state and get one that suits your personal savings.

How to save on auto loans. A smart investor knows he must seize every opportunity that comes knocking at his door - as long as it allows him to save more. Auto refinancing is appealing to those whose credit scores are of good history. This is favorable for a buyer who has no negative records on his account whatsoever.

Auto loans gives the buyer the opportunity to refinance their loan at terms that allows them to save their money. However, refinancing is not saving. At least not what most people deem it to be. Refinancing means reducing monthly payments in order to save a little extra money. Car refinance loans are useful in downsizing.

Auto loans are just a click away, thanks to the Internet. Lenders specializing in refinancing are online to assist possible clients about auto loans. One must submit an application before any negotiation takes place. Provide the same documents required when making a loan at any bank or establishment. But there are auto loan refinances that do not care even if you have a negative credit history. Refinancing at best rates are available if you have a clear record, but that does not mean that because you were a little off in paying at due time, you will not be able to get the auto loan that you are applying for. You still would but the rate won't be as good as opposed to you having a clear record.

Throughout the duration of the loan, there are opportunities to refinance the car loan. If you are opting for refinancing, know that the options for auto loans are negotiated with the lender beforehand.

There can be changes as long as there is the approval from the lender and the person applying for the loan. If you need refinancing as soon as possible, consult with the lender and try to work around auto loan refinancing requirements. By updating yourself with the services and programs offered by the various car refinance loan specialists out there, then you are more aware of which one you should choose - depending on the one that works for you best.

Refinance car loan specialists are more than willing to cooperate with you if the terms you are asking for are favorable for them. The catch is that when you choose to refinance then the rates are lower and you will be able to save more. Auto loan refinancing opens more doors to saving because it reduces your monthly payments at the interest rate of your choice. Here is a tip before you invest in auto loans, what are your goals for refinancing? You have to compare with the other auto refinancing businesses before you fully decide on one. Choose one where you get the best deal and where you will be able to save more. You have a right to do so because it is your money and your investment.

For car owners, investing on auto loans is a wise decision because it gives them better deals. However, before you commit yourself to any refinancing agreement, you have to take into consideration all the terms that are involved in the car financing program you are committing to.

Also, by tapping the equity in your home loan, you will be able to lower the interest payment when buying a car. That is because the home equity loan can actually provide a lower rate as opposed to a car loan. The former is more secured than the latter. You can consult a tax advisor for a second opinion. If you want you can approach an independent lender before you completely decide on which car to purchase. By arranging the terms and finances before buying the car, dealer financers will be able to assist the consumer in which auto loan refinancing can give him the best deal, making him save the most amount.

You must also be very wary of the zero-interest loans. Just like with any other deals, it may sound tempting but that is not usually the case. You may be buying a car for $18,000 and pay zero interest for two years through the dealer and getting a rebate of $3000, but how sure are you that there is no catch on that offer? If you do take the rebate and finance at the given percent, then who knows you may even save more.

Think twice before you make any decision. Especially since it involves money. Stretch your buck for as long as it would take.

How to save on mortgage loans. Save on mortgage loans It is very important to save especially during these tough times. So the best advice anyone can give you is to sign up for the right mortgage loan that is appropriate for your budget.

Mortgage loans are calculated depending on the kind of interest that you signed up for. This is based on the interest rate and the length of mortgage. The shorter the duration of the payment, then the more expensive the bill is on a monthly basis; however, the higher the bill per month, the shorter the time duration of the payment. It's all about the question of how much you can afford. Create a budget and envision, how much can you actually pay in a month. Think long term. Will you still be earning that particular amount in two, three years time? Do you have enough savings just in case an unforeseen accident occurs? How long can you keep on paying the mortgage?

This is how some lenders calculate how much they can lend you. The housing payment is your total mortgage payment set alongside your monthly income and the total debt ratio – meaning what you are obligated to pay in the big picture.

That's why there's also the question of "Should I buy or rent?" If the person isn't yet financially stable, it is better that he rents in the mean time. However, calculations show that the expenditures on rent are somehow close to signing up for a home mortgage.

Also, there's a great sense of pride in owning your own home. But with that comes the responsibility of paying your bills on time. Plus, now that you're a homeowner, you're also required to set aside a significant amount of your salary for taxes. Owning a home also means paying for utilities such as gas, electricity, water and food.

For you to decide, think whether choosing a home is what's suitable for you at this time. Determine if you have enough to actually afford to buy your own home. If not, then it's better that you rent.

Now here's where the mortgage rates come in. Begin by checking the interest rate and rate movements of a specific mortgage loan you're signing up for. Mortgage rates depend on the Wall Street securities. Keep an eye on the stock market and the mortgage market trends to know the secrets on the direction of where your mortgage is going. You must also study the APR or the Annual Percentage Rate.

By law, mortgage companies are required to disclose the APR to their clients. That is how they should advertise a rate. This is done so that people who signed up under them will be aware of where their rates are going. It represents the real cost of the loan to the borrower and can be seen extensively when the yearly rate is presented. This prevents lenders from hiding fees and for clients to have an open relationship with their mortgage dealers.

As much as possible, try to personally meet with the lender. When money is involved, personal arrangements are better because not only can you clarify better, you could also have an idea of what kind the person is on the end of the phone or at the receiving part of the email you send out. Now that you have met up with a dealer, know your APR, study the stock market, and then you are ready to lock in your rate. This means that you are ready to commit with a lender and the lender is bound to a promise to this certain interest rate. From there, you must work on a budget.

You must set aside a specific amount from your salary for your mortgage; and, if you can pay faster, then why not? If you have extra money, talk to your lender and ask if you can pay for a higher amount. For good credit history, always pay more, not less. Pay on time, not late. This is to ensure that you won't have a hard time dealing with insurance matters in the future. With the right decision-making and the right budget, you won't have any problem with money. It's just having the discipline of creating a budget, sticking to it and paying on time. If it is arranged as such, notice that you could even save a couple of your dollars.

How to save on credit cards. The Cost-Effective Ways to Bigger Savings When Times are Tight Statistical reports prove that Americans are in love with plastic.

Consumers know it more as credit cards. In fact, nearly 81% of American households have at least one credit card. They find these plastic as the most convenient tool for shopping and paying utility bills. The credit cards make payments and expenses so convenient that the average credit card balance Americans have amounts to $8,000.

That is, indeed, a great amount of debt. So if you want to avoid debts and save more on your credit card bills, try to cut back on your expenses and follow the rules on how to save on credit cards. Here's how:

1. Choose the best credit card Not all credit cards are created equal. There is a particular credit card that will suit your needs. Getting this type of card will provide you the rewards, services, and interest rates that will suit your needs. For instance, if you want convenient shopping but can't afford to go the extra mile in shopping expenses, it is best to get a credit card that can offer you with reasonable credit limits. In this way, you will not be tempted to max out your card and accumulate debts you simply can't afford to pay.

2. Go for the lowest interest rate If you think you can't pay your credit card bills on time but are willing to pay your balances in another period, it is best to get a credit card with lower interest rates. Consumers may not be aware of this, but one of the reasons why debts are getting higher is based on the interest rates. The actual balances are made worse through interest rate charges.

3. Choose the reward credit cards that suits your lifestyle Don't get a credit card just because it can provide you with several rewards. Not all rewards are worth your time and money. For instance, a frequent flyer's rewards credit card may not be functional if you aren't a frequent traveler. But if you are, getting a flyer's reward credit card can give you discounts as well as points that can be converted into tickets. This will be savings considering the prices of airline tickets nowadays.

4. Keep a record of all your expenses With credit cards, convenience is the name of the game. However, it doesn't necessarily mean that you neglect your responsibilities. One of which is to keep a record of all your expenses. In this way, you will be able to identify which purchases weren't necessary at all. So the next time around, you will know what to avoid.

5. Do not keep balances Never let your balances stay on your credit card bill statements for long. This means that if you have accrued balances for the month, try to pay them immediately. Paying your minimum balance only won't do you any good. In fact,

this might trigger further debts. Besides, interest rates only apply whenever you have balances. And interest rates are additional expenses for you. If you pay your balances monthly, you won't be charged with interest rates, so you get more savings.

6. Be wary of cash advances If it isn't an emergency, never take cash advances on your credit card. Financial experts say that cash advances reap higher interest rates compared to the ones that you have on your credit card purchases, which are, by nature, soaring as well. Combination of these two will definitely bring you to debt problems. Besides, cash advances don't take on certain periods, so that means the charges will take place instantly. That would be very hard if you aren't prepared to pay off your balance immediately.

7. Ask for a lower rate If you have been an obedient customer and pay your bill on time, it wouldn't hurt you to call your bank or your credit card issuer and ask for a lower rate. Surveys show that nearly 55% of those who participated in the survey were reported to have trimmed down their interest rates simply by

requesting their bank or their credit card companies to act accordingly. With lower interest rates, you can definitely save more especially if you are the type of credit card holder who doesn't get to pay the balances on time. All of these things are catered to help you cut back your expenses and save more on your credit cards. These things have been proven effective. It is now up to you if you will heed this advice or not. Just remember, your actions will always tell you the kind of life you want to live, so better make good choices and start saving now.

How to save on gasoline. Managing Oil Prices: Tips on How to Save on Gasoline.

If you have been spending more than what you can afford on your gasoline consumption, you should trim down the refills. There are many things that are more important than just gasoline, so it goes to show that your money shouldn't revolve on your gasoline bills alone.

Saving on gasoline won't necessarily mean commuting and using your car less often in the same way as not eating food just to save on groceries. That is simply not saving.

Saving on gas would mean maximizing the amount of gasoline you use, thus, giving you better gasoline mileage.

Moreover, with the pries of gasoline nowadays, saving more and maximizing your consumption would definitely give you more than what you have paid for. If you think you can't do away without driving and without using gasoline, you just have to learn how to maximize your gasoline consumption and save more. Here are a few reminders:

1. A regular tune up on your car can do wonders A regularly tuned up car will not only mean longer life span of the vehicle but can also guarantee better gas mileage. You don't have to drive the newest model just to ensure better gas mileage. The performance will entirely depend on how you maintain your car's condition. If everything is working quite perfectly, you can be sure that you get better gas mileage, which means less gasoline refills.

2. Are you a racer? If not, then try to drive a little slower. Driving faster than the wind won't only get you into trouble but can also waste a lot of gasoline without you knowing it. Experts say that "traveling velocity" can put a great impact on your gasoline use. For example, if you drive at 105kph instead of 88kph, you are increasing your gasoline consumption up to 17%. That is a lot of gasoline you have there, and when converted into dollars, that is simply overspending.

3. Be wary of your filter's condition Filters may seem one of the most neglected parts on a car. Most motorists don't understand the importance of air filters. Filters make your car's engine more cost-effective. It can create more force and energy and, of course, better gasoline consumption. If your car has a dirty or congested air filter, replacing them will absolutely perk up your car's gasoline mileage up to 10% more. Besides, having clean air filters all the time will ensure your car engine's optimum performance and durability.

4. Break it more gently Breaking and accelerating more frequently will not only wear out your car's condition and tires but can also increase you gasoline consumption more than 18%. So whenever you are on the road, try not to accelerate more than what is recommended. Try to anticipate, as well, the traffic ahead so that you can apply measured, steady brake.

5. Check your tires If your tires are deflating more whenever you drive, you are actually taking more money from your pockets. Why? Simply because the less efficient your tires are, the more gasoline you use, and not just because they deteriorate faster. It is best to always keep your tires well inflated according to the manufacturer's instructions. Keep in mind that a tire that has been inflated by 2 PSI can actually boost your car's gas use by 1%.

6. Organize your shopping trips Getting things organized not only makes life easier to bear but can also save more on your expenses. Consider this: try to budget your food consumption for the week and have all your groceries bought on a single day. It would be best if you can find all of the things you

need in a single store. In this way, you can cut back on fuel use.

7. Reduce wind resistance If you will be driving on a highway, it is best to keep your windows closed so as to lessen that drag. Dragging can aggravate fuel consumption. Remember your physics? It will definitely take more force just to push your car through the wind and this would mean using more gas than usual. All of these things can, in some way or another, help you save on gas. Just try to be conscious of where your money goes and it will be easier for you to find cost-effective ways to save more money.

How to save on car repairs. The Car Owner's Ultimate Guide Book to Savings Are you one of those few people who are having trouble in getting their cars repaired and drain their finances as well? If you are, then it is high time you start looking for ways to save on car repairs and save more in your piggy bank.

Defective cars aren't even worthy to be sold without getting all the necessary repairs. You can't even exchange it with another car without getting it repaired. You are left with no choice at all but to get it fixed. The only problem is that without the appropriate guidelines you need in choosing the right repairs, you can be spending more than what you can afford.

With the high prices going on in the market today, no one can really afford to have their cars repaired in very expensive packages. So you have to think of ways to save more on car repairs. You can trim down on car repairs and save more cash on an ordinary basis without opting to excessive ways. Here's how you can save on car repairs:

1. Do your homework One of the greatest problems most motorists encounter is that they spend more on car repairs simply because they didn't choose the best mechanic or repair service for their cars. Through research, you can identify the right mechanic and the right shop.

2. Take note of the things that need to be repaired Before you go to your mechanic, it is best to have all the necessary repairs listed on a piece of paper. In

this way, you can tell your mechanic right way the things that need to be repaired. This will prevent unnecessary repairs or misunderstandings on the type of repairs that your car needs. Unnecessary repairs will only add up to your repair expenses.

3. Shop and compare To get the best quotes on car repairs, try to shop around and compare prices. In this way, you can evaluate and compare prices enabling you to find the best quotes possible. Never grab the first repair shop you find. By looking around, you can still find better shops than what you have right now.

4. Try to make every transaction in black and white This means that before you commit yourself in a particular repair job, it is best to have the estimate written on a piece of paper. Try to acquire a copy of your own. This will prevent unnecessary accumulation of extra charges, which weren't included on the first estimation. Keep in mind that not all job repairs were created equal and not all mechanics are honest. So it is best to protect yourself as always.

5. Acquire your car's old parts before you let the mechanic start the repair process There are certain car parts that can still be rebuilt. So never let your mechanic take the chance of acquiring these things. You can have them repaired on some machine shops and cut back your expenses on the next repair.

6. Know your way around If you don't know your way around car repairs, it is best to ask someone (definitely not your mechanic) for some second opinions. In this way, you can decide which things need greater considerations. Besides, if you will just let your mechanic decide on your car's repair process, you might pay more than what you can imagine. Better yet, read some easy-to-read manuals on car maintenance. In this way, you will learn some important matters regarding car parts. This will enable you to differentiate the important repairs from those that you can do by yourself.

7. Ask for the warranty Some repair shops offer warranties on the services that they make. Take note of this so that you can be sure not to spend another hundred dollars for the same repair in just a few days.

Furthermore, warranties can guarantee high quality repairs so you can be sure that your car and your pocket are in good hands. Indeed, car repairs can't be avoided. These are the things that you have to learn to live with. Finding good repair shops aren't that hard. Just try to remember these pointers and you will surely spend less with car repairs.

Also, think about learning how to do the simple chores yourself. That's where those manuals may come in handy. With just a little bit of knowledge you can handle minor maintenance like oil changes, tune-ups, changing windshield wipers and other simple tasks. Learning to do these yourself will result in great savings!

How to save on home improvement. Have you ever thought of changing your room's design? Do you think your porch needs a little makeover? Then it is time for you to make some improvements in your home and create a difference.

Home improvement can add sparkle to a dull wall color, a new shade to a dreary interior design, or vigor to a lifeless porch. It simply pertains to the method of refurbishing or repairing a home. In most cases, an expert executes home improvements.

However, with the cost of commodities nowadays, plus the real service fees of "professional handyman," many people have opted to work on their home improvements through their own initiative. No wonder why the so-called "do-it-yourself" jobs have been pretty popular. Through this process, homeowners can enjoy renovating their own homes like professionals.

There are shops that provide seminars or workshops regarding their products and the way homeowners can operate them at home. There are many types of home improvements. Each category can provide optimum modernization to one's home.

However, home improvement package prices may vary. It is best to identify the right measures to save more on home improvements. Here are some ways on how to cut back on your home improvement costs:

1. Do your research Before you start on your home improvement project, it is best to do some extensive research. Try to find out the current prices of home improvement packages available on the market today. It is also best to identify the different factors that can affect the conditions of each type of home improvements.

2. Scout for the best quotes If you will be hiring a professional, it is best to look for the best price quotes on home improvements. In this way, you will be able to anticipate the possible rates and charges, which will enable you to prepare the required amount. Get quotes from more than one tradesman.

3. Do the math Before you start buying things that you need for your home improvement, it is best to have everything estimated. Should you decide to seek the services of a professional you will know how much it will take you to improve your home. You can't easily be fooled by anyone because you know exactly the cost of expenses. Besides, having a rough estimate of your home improvement plans will enable you to control your expenses. You can focus on the areas

that need to be prioritized. Once you have set a specific budget on it, you can now consider the other areas without having to spend more than what you can afford.

4. Decide whether you can do it yourself or you should hire a professional If you want to save more on your home improvements, it is best to decide if you can do the project yourself or you really need to hire a professional. It is unwise to assume that you can do the job just to trim down your expenses, where in fact, you don't have the slightest idea how to start the job. Insisting to do the job yourself will only end up in waste or destruction. It is best to hire a professional if you really want to save on your home improvement.

5. Ask for recommendations Word of mouth is considered as one of the best advertising strategy in marketing. It is also one of the best ways to ask for some help about the things that you are not familiar with. For example, if you don't have any idea about home improvements, it is best to ask your friends, relatives, or even colleagues about home improvements. They can give you some pointers

about home improvements based on their own experience. Tried and tested, their idea about home improvements can really help you make a difference.

6. Find the best contractor If you wish to save on home improvements through contractors, it is best to hire the best. You can do this by checking on your contractor's capabilities and certifications. In this way, you can be sure that the services you pay are reliable and efficient. Try to keep these things in mind to save on your home improvement projects. Keep in mind that home improvements need not be expensive. You can beautify your home without having to go overboard.

How to save on home heating and energy. Superb Saving Ideas To say that you can save on your home's heating system and energy isn't an understatement. Reduced bills on your electricity, maximized heating system, and a whole lot of energy saving phenomenon are things you don't see everyday but desire to obtain. Everybody longs to reduce his or her expenses on energy and heating systems. People don't work just to pay the utility bills alone.

The greatest reason for this dilemma is the on-going increase of energy consumption charges. Everything seems to have high prices nowadays. It is best to trim down the other expenses in which you have control of, such as energy consumption.

One of the best examples of energy use are home heating systems. However, heaters can eat up bigger portions in your electricity bill. In fact, statistical reports prove that heaters are one of the largest energy consumers in every home, that is, more than half of the consumption rate in a given year.

For this reason, it is imperative to think of ways to save on heating systems so as to save on energy consumption as well. As you save on these items, you get more value for your money. But how? Things are, most of the time, easier said than done. So if you think that it is easy to maximize your heaters and save more on energy, think again.

To help you, here is a list of some energy saving tips that will help you cut back on your furnaces' energy consumption.

1. Use solar energy Natural is always the best. To save more on energy, it is best to use solar energy when using water heaters in your home's heating system. In this way, you trap natural heat coming from the sun. You will consume less energy. With the solar energy utilized in your home's heating system, you can start heating your water for showers or revolutionize your home's heating system and still reduce your electricity bill.

2. Inspect your home To maximize your home's heating system, it is best to inspect your house for any leakage. Leaks will let the heat seep out from your home, thus, absorbing cold from the outside. Most of the areas that leakage starts to develop are in the windows, doors, and fireplaces. Once identified, it is best to take some proper actions as soon as possible so as to cut back any unnecessary costs on energy.

3. Use heaters on frequently used rooms only To save more energy, only use heaters on areas that are frequently visited and used by your household. For rooms that are not being used, try to turn off the thermostat or close the windows to utilize natural heat. Close the vents to the rooms that you are not using. By doing so, you can cut back your energy consumption through your furnace by as much as 50%.

4. Insulate One of the biggest secrets in maximizing your home's heating system is insulation. A properly and well insulated home can guarantee a comfortable home without using too much energy. Thus, you can save more money by cutting back your energy consumption. It is best to use some insulating devices on your roof, windows, and other areas that need padding. This will block the heat in and keep it from escaping the house.

5. Get a good heating system Of course, you can never guarantee lower energy bill if not for an efficient heating system. A defective heating system can use twice as much energy as one that is functioning

properly. The tendency is to use more force just to boost more heat, and the more force the heating device use, the more energy it will consume. Besides, defective products would require frequent visits to repair shops and that would be additional expenses for you. All of these things can help you maximize your heating system and save more energy. In this way, you can save more money and use it on other things that need prioritization.

Depending on where you live, consider switching from electric to gas or vice versa. Electricity is less costly in some areas while in other areas gas is the better choice. Do your research for the area you live in and determine which better meets your needs.

How to save on phone service. Since its inception, long distance calls have created a niche in the telecommunications industry in the United States. In fact, reports from the Federal Communications Commission have attested that more than 1.75% of consumers' general expenses are attributed to phone services such as long distance calls.

No wonder why many Americans are squanderers when it comes to phone services. In 1992, reports show that the average amount that the Americans spend on long distance calls amount to $10.3 billion. Now, the question lies on whether these expenses are maintained and paid by the phone companies' subscribers.

Come to think of it, the utilization of phone services has increased to a level where consumers can no longer pay their dues. What happens next is that some phone companies were required to make some cutbacks on their operating expenses. But to some, cutbacks aren't the ultimate solution. Most of the phone companies have come up with revolutionary added features that are more functional and multidimensional.

These items seek to entice people to subscribe to phone services once more and gain back the popularity that the phone companies used to have. With these phone companies have created different choices for long distance calls. Each feature is designed to suit the needs of every customer or subscriber. The usual phone service options are the bundled, traditional, VoIP, wireless, and calling cards. Each service has its own pros and cons, but all of them were catered to provide optimum phone services to their subscribers. Sounds good enough? Think again.

With the high prices of commodities nowadays, it pays a lot to save on your phone services and earn that extra money you will need in the near future. But how? First, keep in mind that not all phone services were created equal. And even if they may vary according to their rates and charges, consumers can find ways on how to save on phone services, regardless of their classification and the type of service that they provide.

Here are some few good tips:

1. Select a good plan To save more on your phone services, it is best to choose a good plan first. You can do this by checking on the phone companies available on the market today. Compare their rates and choose the best plan. However, experts say that

it would be better if you choose from the three leading phone companies in the industry. Statistical reports show that you can save by as much as 50% or more as compared to other phone companies.

2. Identify your "calling pattern" Try to identify your calling pattern based on the latest three bills. Analyze the flow of calls and pinpoint those that create particular patterns. Once you have identified them, you can easily detect which areas you call frequently, at what time, and for how long. So if you have clearly identified your calling pattern," it will be easier for you to save more on your bills.

3. Flexibility Choose a phone service that gives you the flexibility to adapt to your needs. This will guarantee optimum communication service because you can alter or modify any feature that will correspond to your needs. For example, if you have been previously subscribed to a postpaid long distance phone service and you wish to convert your phone service into prepaid, it is best to choose a long distance carrier that will allow you to do such thing without the extra charges. In this way, you can save

on the service fees (for the conversion) as well as on the long distance charges. With prepaid, you can now control your long distance activities.

4. Be wary on the promotions Not all freebies and promotions can be good for you. There are some promotions that may only lure to try a particular phone service, only to find out that you get double charges in return after the promotion is over. With this, you not only passed the chance of saving more money on your phone services, but you also missed the chance to enjoy real savings without having to spend more than what you can afford. Indeed, saving on phone services can trim down your expenses in a month. It is best to remember these pointers very well as they may come in handy sometime in the future.

How to save on major appliances. Saving is one of the most important things to consider in budgeting. Whether you are a parent of two or three or a student or an independent planning to move to a different place, saving should always be put as a number one priority. For example, moving into a new area requires basic household appliances such as fridge, washing machine, stove, and heater.

Normally, these appliances would cost you thousands of dollars if one would not consider some of the cost-effective tips in buying major appliances. With that being said, below are just some of the cost-effective and saving tips in purchasing new appliances for your new abode.

a. Evaluate your Wants and Needs. Appliances will always be part of our daily lives but with a starter, one would have to evaluate and think about the most important household appliances to buy. First, think about the things that you should need when moving to a new house. Would you prefer buying a fridge in favor of a new sofa or a convenient ice-making machine against a reasonable fridge? While these add-ons are important, this should also require a lot of thinking in order to keep all those that are important and set aside those that will provide luxury. Worth mentioning is the amount of electricity that one has to consume when using these add-on products.

b. Size – accommodating your newly purchased electrical appliances can be fun if you have enough or available space. It isn't wise to purchase a huge refrigerator when you only have few square inches of space available for your immediate kitchen needs.

For families, parents should also take into consideration the type of appliances, which will be able to supply all the needs for the family. A 5.0-kilogram washer would definitely not suffice in a family of 5. In such cases, one would have to consider purchasing those that are of heavy-duty type of major appliances. You will save more on buying in bulk than for one that won't accommodate most of the clothing used for a week by a single person alone.

c. Consult with Comparison Shops. The 1999 Consumer Literacy Consortium report provides enough reason for consumers to compare price around before they do the actual purchasing on major appliances. Basically, for people who are determined to make the purchase, they would usually shop on a single appliance center and don't bother to shop around and compare prices at nearby stores.

The consumer report provided information about the benefits of comparing prices on the market before doing the actual buying and the importance of shopping online for auctions and sales.

More often than not, leveraging on secondhand appliances is better than procuring a new one specially when one would look into similar features and durability standard. This intelligent buying will save you hundreds of dollars as expected and allot savings to other home stuffs that in turn provides additional luxury in your part.

d. Annual Buying Guide – Local libraries today keep some records of buying guides and ratings and prices on some of the major appliances nationwide. These buying guides and consumer literacy reports provide exclusive and substantial information on performance (durability), price, and quality among other things. The report also maintains a database where you can compare prices from coast to coast and details on handling and packaging of merchandises should one would interest on buying them.

e. Where to Buy – Sometimes, it isn't about the name of the merchandiser that matters when filling your home with major appliances. It's about how you would search the local market and the net to find shopping exclusives and sales of appliance items whose features and performance match specifically to the needs and wants of your family.

These buying techniques won't only free you on your budget but provide you additional leverage on saving for future appliance needs.

f. Negotiate – In almost every part of the selling process, negotiation takes place when you would interest on purchasing the item after making a careful review of its features. Getting the best bet lies in your ability to making compromises. Most stores would drop prices when needed and when the customer asks for it and when one is purchasing refurbished items.

How to save on furniture. Saving money on purchasing your furniture for your home doesn't necessarily mean sacrificing the quality of the product.

Of course, you want only the best worth for your very own home. The following are keys and tips that you can follow to save an awful lot of money when you procure your dream furniture:

1. Look for Furniture on SALE! More often than not, the best deal on Furniture on Sale comes every January and July. And if you're looking for outdoor furniture, August is the best time ever! Also, most of the furniture companies have their furniture set on very low prices every end of the month for sole purpose of their clearance. Majority of the retail furniture companies function on monthly basis, computing their sales, releasing their promotions and introducing new furniture.

This means that at the end of the month, there will be certain pieces of furniture that won't be offered the following month, thus these lines of products will be offered at a very low price. Another reason will be because most of the furniture companies hire sales people and pay them by commission. These people will definitely have their own bills to pay so would be a little more desperate to make the sale, hence, could be giving a better deal for your most wanted furniture. You can definitely take advantage of their eagerness.

2. Visit your Favorite Furniture Stores Check all the possible Furniture Shops first and find the best deal before finally purchasing your piece. Most regional and national furniture retailers have outlet shops where suspended, distressed and returned merchandise is being sold at low prices. Form a habit of checking these shops frequently —you never know when the right furniture is going to be waiting for you at its best deal!

3. Apply for the Credit Card being offered by the Furniture Shop Some wholesale furniture shops offer in-store credit cards. These credit cards normally give you the best discounts on the furniture inside that furniture center.

All you have to do is apply for this credit card and you can get discounts for your desired piece of fixture.

Then, you may pay for your credit card bill the following day using the money that you have allotted for the furniture; this will save you the finance charge that the credit card company may cost you.

4. Search the World Wide Web After seeing a certain piece of furniture either at the store near you or in a certain magazine, check the Net for this certain product. Just enter the manufacturer's name and if that piece has its name as well. Use the famous search engines like Google and Yahoo.

There are some Online Shops that may offer your certain furniture at a very good discount. However, it is imperative to check the shipping rates and taxes that may be applied with the product. Please don't just rely on the price that is posted on the initial site for it may mislead you on possible additional charges.

5. Go Directly To The Manufacturer If you live within a few miles of a furniture manufacturer, it is strongly suggested that you visit their shops for you may get the lowest possible price for your preferred furniture.

6. Buy Used Furniture One of the best ways of saving your hard-earned money is by going to Secondhand shops for certain furniture. You may opt to have your fixture reupholstered or refinished by your favorite carpenter to put the touch of your individuality and giving it the smell of novelty.

More often than not, the total price of your furniture plus the cost of the repair is still a lot cheaper than buying a totally new piece. Stores selling used furniture are almost everywhere especially in major cities.

How to save on clothing. Clothes can be really costly, especially when all the fads and trends come and go as the seasons. It is very possible to save money when buying your clothes.

You just need to have the strategies and tactics on how you can save your money. Here are some tips on how to save when buying your clothes: Don't buy in Season clothes – different line of clothes come every season. And more often than not, they normally release new clothes at very high prices and normally they go down after a few months. Key is just patience to wait. For example, when winter comes, coats and sweaters are released, however, after a month, normal Sale or bargain prices will now be tagged on these clothes.

If you were smart enough to wait, you can still wear these clothes during the remaining days of winter and the coming fall.

· Wait for Factory Sales – when Factories put out their sale season, clothes can be cut from 40%-90% off the original price. Imagine how big this saving is! Also, going directly to the Manufacturer's store is a helpful tip on getting a good deal on clothes.

· Garage Sales – these are very popular stores and places where you can get your clothes at really, really low prices. Find garage sales that are put up by families, in this way, chances of getting quality clothes are much higher than those garage sales that have been put up for commercial purposes already. However, it is important to remember and avoid buying clothes just because the prices are really low, you might not even wear the clothes, and the concept of saving is put to waste.

· Bargain – always visit your favorite store and befriend the sales people there. You can then ask for the possible dates of SALE and bargain wherein you can save at a minimum of 20% off the original price of your desired clothes.

· Buy two different sizes and two different colors – If you have kids, it is very advisable to actually get two sizes, since children grow up really fast. Also, buying two colors to have variety, only if the clothes are already at their reduced rates.

· Shop Online – nowadays, there are many clothing stores online. And most of the clothing lines have their own websites where you can online shop. Like the regular stores, the online shops have their season for SALE and BARGAINS as well. Just make a habit of checking regularly your favorite clothing line to wait for these awaited bargains.

· Sign up for your Favorite Boutique's mailing list – be sure to sign up for your favorite clothing store's mailing list, newsletter and catalogs. In this way, you will be updated and be the first one to know of the upcoming On Sale Items and the new releases of the trendy clothes as well.

· Coupon Codes and Coupon Cards – if shopping online is your thing, there are many coupon codes that can be found online that could give you a cut off of the original price of your favorite online store. Some of the coupon code sites are the www.couponcabin.com and www.keycode.com. All you have to do is look for the "apparel" category code and you will be given your choices of retailers.

You can also put the "online coupon" or "coupon code" in your favorite search engines such as Google and you will be given a list of sites that could provide you best deals for your retailers.

· In-Store Credit Cards – many boutiques nowadays, offer in-store credit cards. All you need to do is apply for a credit card of your own, especially if you have a favorite store where you frequently buy your clothes.

Normally, these credit cards give good discounts on clothes being sold in that particular boutique.

Also, the cardholders normally get special coupons, birthday discounts and other relative discounts every holiday and often you can get a minimum of 5% up to 15% discounts. Another benefit of these is free shipping, being updated of the new arrival of clothes and rebates. However, this tactic only is beneficial if you plan to pay your credit card bill a day after you have purchased the product. This is because credit card companies charge an awful lot of finance fees and interests. It may not even counterbalance the savings you intentionally wanted in applying for the credit card.

· Get a part-time job at your favorite store – a lot of shoppers apply and get part time jobs on their favorite boutique. This will give them extra money for their job and employee's discounts on the clothes being sold in that particular store.

How to save on groceries. One of the basic necessities is your stock of groceries. And your budget for the groceries could make or break your budget for your weekly funds that should be allotted on other things.

This is how flexible the budget for the groceries could be. This flexibility should be handled properly. Here are tips on how you can save money for your groceries:

· Make sure you aren't hungry before you go to the Grocery Store – studies have shown that shoppers tend to buy more in the grocery stores when they are hungry. This is the reason why some grocery shops have their bakery along the entrance of the store.

The smell of the freshly baked breads and cakes could really make you hungry. And this could make you shop and spend more than what you intended. The best way to handle this is to make sure your stomach is not empty, if no food can be taken; drink at least a glass or two of water. Shopping when you're full will help you combat the temptations of the mouth-watering smells inside the grocery store.

· Try to look up and down on the shelves – make sure that you search the higher and lower shelves. The more expensive brands are normally located on the shelves on your chest level. The cheaper or generic brands are either located below or higher than your average sight.

· Shop alone – try to find time to go to the grocery store by yourself. When you ask for helpers, they tend to increase your bill.

· Go to the store at the early time of the day – when you go to the grocery store early in the morning, you tend to finish with your list a little faster, thus avoiding the need to roam around and get attracted to unnecessary expenses.

· Shop when you are in a good mood – when you shop and you feel tired, you tend to buy more sweets, chocolates and high carbohydrates. And when you are mad, you tend to buy more junk food. Don't buy non-grocery items – grocery stores normally sell some non-grocery items like contact lens and painkillers. These products normally cost more at the grocery stores.

· Always bring your calculator – make sure to shop with your calculator. In this way, you can easily compute how much you save when buying in-packs or individually wrapped items.

· Check your receipts after shopping, mistakes can happen no matter how much you avoid them. Remember that every cent counts. Buy foods that are fresh, cheap and seasoned. With fewer dealers involved, the cheaper, fresher and better quality of food that you can get for your family.

Make sure to double-check the weights of the pre-packed goodies that you buy. Sometimes they lack a little pound or weigh less than what they normally should. Make it a point that you get all your hard-earned money's worth. When you specifically went to your favorite grocery shop for a definite item on sale and suddenly knowing that it's no longer available.

Make sure that you make a rain check and ask for the next stocks to arrive. So that you'll be early the next time the stocks reach the store.

· Check the ends and edges of the grocery store. More often than not, the healthy and fresher foods are located at the ends of the grocery shops. Fruits, vegetables, Dairy products and meats are examples of these. Avoid walking thru the main areas, since these regions are normally where the products are very expensive and cost more. It's important to focus on the price of the item. Make sure to check the other brands to be certain of getting the best deal.

Also, buy only what you need. Sometimes, you get deceived when you get to buy things that are on sale even if you don't need them. If this happens, you didn't get the bargain no matter how cheap it seemed.

Don't be misled with the brilliant colored packaging of the grocery shops. They normally pack certain items simply to attract. Focus on your list and buy things that you need.

How to save on vacations. Save on your Vacations It is true that after all saving and cutting down all the expenses from other things like clothes, appliances and groceries, you and your family deserves a well planned vacation at least once a year. However, it is still imperative to save as much as you can while having your vacation.

Especially, while you are on vacation, more often than not, the budget is a tough thing to keep. Here are the ways on how you can save on your vacations: Save on Airfares – Make arrangements and book your flights ahead of time. Airlines normally have promos if you purchase your tickets in advance. Also, Airline tickets sell evening flights a little cheaper than those of the day flights. If you are purchasing your Airline tickets from the travel agencies in your area, make sure to scout for the best deal for ticket prices.

When buying tickets for your family or for four or more passengers, there will be special discounts, be sure to ask for these opportunities to save.

· If possible, plan your vacation during the off-peak seasons. The travel agency has its peak and off-peak seasons. Make sure to research these dates. Every destination has its own determination of peak seasons. Airfares and hotel accommodation are much cheaper during the lean seasons. Make sure to bring packaged snacks that are purchased at supermarkets.

Eating and dining out in restaurants can be really expensive especially if you are traveling in groups. For road/land trips, as much as possible, bring your own car for your tour. Car rentals can be really expensive and unnecessary.

Don't forget an auto-check up from your favorite and trusted mechanic before leaving for vacation. Don't forget to fill your gas tank. This will allow you to shop for cheap gasoline stations and avoid unplanned stops along the way. Don't pay for your vacation in credit unless you are very certain that you can pay on time. Interests on such credit can be a burden especially after having fun on your vacation.

Don't forget to turn off ongoing expenses while you're away on vacation. Discontinue your newspaper deliveries. Temporarily cancel your internet service when on vacation for more than a month. Turn off your gas and electric heater when you are away from home.

· Planning in advance can help you save with your budget. Prepare proper clothes to bring for the destination. Buying emergency clothes for cold climate can be really costly and should be avoided since you can pack all these from home. In this way, you can spend your vacation money on other important things. Always keep your receipts and track your records for all the expenses during the vacation.

These can help for future vacations and can also be deductibles for taxes if you are on business trips.

· Plan for your Accommodation – considering homes of relatives or close friends can help you save on your vacation. You can also choose paid accommodations with cooking facilities. This can help you save money from eating out at restaurants. Take advantage of special offers from hotels or motels offering "family" rates. Be sure to take advantage of free tourist attractions such as parks, museums, free gardens and monuments.

· Consider an adventure trip or "camping" vacation. This is really cheap and fun. Some national parks and forest campgrounds only charge you minimal fee for your stay, and some even let you rent your tents. The idea of marshmallows with hotdogs on your bonfire can be really exiting.

Don't forget to budget your money for your souvenir allowance. Don't buy unnecessary souvenir items that can only be sold at your garage sale the following year. Buy something useful. Be sure to have portable irons when traveling. Press jobs at the hotels are really expensive. Don't forget to bring your first aid kit that should contain, medicines, alcohol, and stuffs that can heal minor bruises and cuts.

· Leave and entrust your pets to your friends or families instead of bringing them along.

How to save on prescription drugs. There are many money-saving tips in purchasing prescription drugs and one way to doing this is to go through all your resources and look into other possibilities which will help you accomplish the task on saving.

A recent national study on prescription drugs show that most Americans are using more prescription drugs at a younger age. Oftentimes, people resorted to ineffective medical products in favor of more potent yet approved products by the government.

The study revealed that the Americans spending have increased to twenty five percent annually between 1996 and 1999. The same thing applies to seniors. It shows that more than fifty percent of the senior citizens aren't covered by any insurance inclusive of medicine benefits specifically for prescription drugs.

The following tips provides the best recommendations for saving on prescription drugs and how one would be able to manage to keep them fresh and save on future need of such drugs.

a) Go for Generics - Don't forget to request the generic brand of the drug prescribed to you. Up to fifty percent or more can be saved from the cost of the initially prescribed medicine by your doctors. Using the generic brand of medicine can help you save on the average cost of each medicine. Most pharmacies don't offer generic brands unless specifically asked.

b) Make Comparisons - Make sure to compare the prices from different pharmacies before finally purchasing. Values can really vary. Some pharmacies can offer certain discounts on specific brands of medicines.

c) Look for Discounts - Members of AARP can receive discounts especially from mail-order pharmacy discounts. Check the Veterans Administration to check if you are eligible for some veterans' benefits.

d) Keep Drugs Away from Sunlight. Make sure to store your medicines and pills away from moisture and heat to ensure the optimal potency of these drugs. Most drugs, when exposed to sunlight, tend to lose their potency. This happens because the very chemical nature of the drug is destroyed and thereby losing its original chemical effect on the body.

e) Talk to your Doctor - It is definitely okay to ask and inquire to your doctors about the medicines prescribed to you. You are still in control of your own health. And most doctors even expect you to ask for less expensive brands of the medicines written on your prescriptions. You are the only one responsible for your health; it is necessary that you are well informed of all the medicines and medications you are taking.

f) Assess yourself - It is imperative to keeping a daily "record" of your physical health. It is really easy to research on your medical condition over the Internet. Maximize your resources. Comply with the treatment plan that you and your physician have designed for your health. Carefully and specifically following this plan can help you save money and avoid future recurrence of the existing illness.

g) Double it Up - The fastest way to saving money is by dividing the drug cost in half. One way to do this is through literally cutting a drug in half to attain the exact dosage desired. For example, if your doctor prescribed you a 40 mg dosage, you can buy the 80 mg tablet and just split it in half. This is since there is a very minimal difference on the price of the 40 mg to the 80 mg. You can save by doing this technique.

h) Ask for the samples. A lot of pharmaceutical companies supply their pharmacies with more than enough of sample medicines. They are very eager to let people try their products. All you have to do is ask your pharmacists. This can be really safe for short-term illnesses, and could help you save money before buying.

i) Know what your medical insurance covers. Make sure that you fully understand its coverage before signing up with the plan. Be specific of the maximum amount of your co-payments will pay for the whole year. More often than not, a health plan only approves for certain pre-approved drugs. Don't forget to consult your family doctor before completely signing up for the plan. Open formularies present more drugs but cost of the plan will definitely vary.

j) It costs less to buy your medicine in bulk. However, make sure to discuss this with your physician, some medicines aren't advisable to be purchased in bulk.

EXTRA

Confusions About Passive Income

If you already got here then you already realized that there's another way of living where you can create your lifestyle by creating your world, your environment and your source of income, in struggling to find a job and die of boredom doing the same year after a year for a salary that will not grow until you grow old and die, probably without a penny in your pocket, old and sick, and also very lonely for sure.

By creating passive income, you can live without a schedule required by a boss and work from anywhere in the world while your income continues to be produced day after day.

But, here comes the great "But", there are very few who manage to turn that dream into reality, because it depends on several intangible factors that all reside in your mind and on the power you may have to dominate them because in reality they are all disciplinary factors, habits you can create or remove, and that my friend depends on you, and that's where those mix-ups come from, let's start;

Lack of Belief

Everything that looks like earning money from the internet and that looks like residual income sounds like a mirage, a Chinese tale and a scam, and here many already give up because they prefer money earned with the sweat of their forehead day after day, but yes, "yes they pay me work ", and that is linear money, so these people aren't made to live the emotion of building passive income.

And it's that these types of people have a hard time seeing that the effort you are putting today will not be immediately rewarded, this will be paid after several attempts, and it can be many until you get the right mechanism according to the type of passive income you are looking to seek utility.

As logical as every one of the strategies described here may seem, the truth is that most people don't believe they are capable of creating and developing them, and here a lot are left out of the game, so they are waiting for you. a long working day for about 40 years.

I recommend these books;

Believe It to Achieve It: Overcome Your Doubts, Let Go of the Past, and Unlock Your Full Potential
Brian Tracy

Unlimited Power: The New Science Of Personal Achievement
Tony Robbins

Lack of Action

Here we find a group of brave and dreamers who if they believe they can build passive income but never finish launching any project, are very afraid of failing and spend hours thinking about details to start some passive income adventure but paralyzed by the fear of just think that they may neglect the job they have and lose it because they are thinking about financial freedom, running out of bread and cheese. Since no idea that occurs to them seems like an absolute winning idea, they stay there, as dreamers.

Others in this category spend months designing the perfect plan and spend months adjusting details, precisely because they don't finish visualizing or clicking on their winning idea.

I give you something, don't wait for the winning idea, what I recommend is to make attempts, it begins, that's all, you try, you must take steps forward, along the way you can make adjustments, otherwise you will never start, and only like this You will be able to learn, because in everything I have done none but none of my ideas have worked for me in the first one, all of them have produced me after months of making adjustments testing niches, investing time and money, and in other cases it simply has not worked and I've had to move on to other ideas.

Get moving and act.

Without Discipline nothing happens

We go for the third group, which believes it and has also decided to take action and take its first risky steps, but does not have the necessary Discipline to keep persisting and make attempts after attempts, adjustments after adjustments to achieve the desired result, simply he starts, makes several attempts and gives up because he has a hard time fighting against frustration.

Let me tell you that Discipline is a significant factor of success. You should definitely know that to succeed you must decide to get up every day to make your ideas work, think about how to make it work, shape it, make attempts, don't give up, put your thinking 100% positive and shout to the universe that you will not give up until the objective is surrendered at your feet. Of course, here too a lot roll and return to their jobs running before they can lose it.

I recommend several books that can help you with different factors of Discipline and perseverance;

"Shoe Dog: A Memoir by the Creator of Nike"
Phil Knight

"The Monk Who Sold His Ferrari: A Fable About Fulfilling Your Dreams & Reaching Your Destiny"
Robin Sharman

"Think and Grow Rich"
Napoleon Hill

"Think Big: Make It Happen in Business and Life"
Donald Trump

"The Power of Focus: What the World's Greatest Achievers Know about The Secret to Financial Freedom & Success"
Jack Canfild

Creating Passive Income Really Isn't Easy

This is so, creating passive income isn't easy, all the strategies described here require time and dedication, and in some cases also require capital investment, so you must create your sources of passive income without haste, without stress and with maturity, otherwise you will feel suffocated and you will surrender without having won a single dollar before.

You can never place all your hopes in a source of passive income that you are designing, in fact if you study the great millionaires you will realize that as they grow in capital they are always looking for where to move and create new sources of passive income to diversify their investments and alternatives, that is why you have to create several sources of residual income and the intention is to be able always to keep making money in various markets; if oil goes down, if a hurricane comes, if the cost of medicine goes up, if the stock market plummets, if real estate falls apart, if a war breaks out in the Middle East, if anything happens, it doesn't matter because you you have your sources of passive income diversified.

So long hours without sleep await you, much to think about, many attempts ahead, struggling with frustration, perhaps with the ridicule of your friends, percent, many of them will look for you to borrow money once they see you earn money , traveling and having a good quality of life, and never think that creating sources of passive income is blowing and bottle-making or rubbing Aladdin's lamp and waiting for the genie to appear and fulfill all your wishes and suddenly overnight. Tomorrow you will get rich.

See you at the world's airports.

THE BIG SECRET - SELF-CONTROL

- if you control yourself,
you control the money –

"I have missed more than 9,000 shots in my career. I have lost almost 300 games. 26 times they have trusted me to take the shot that won the game and I failed. I have failed over and over again in my life and that is why I succeed."

Michael Jordan

A person who does not know how to control his emotions is simply incapable of getting the money into his hands, and if the money comes through a coup de grace then he will lose it at any moment as a result of losing control of his feelings and thoughts that finally provoke an emotion that will lead him to make mistakes, his mind is simply not prepared to receive, retain and multiply money, therefore, he sabotages himself to avoid living with that burden, with the responsibility that comes with money.

Do you feel like you're losing control of yourself? Are you ready to take charge of your own life? By being in charge of your own life you will feel more powerful. Many times people find that they are allowing other people to take charge of their lives. Sometimes it is easy to fall into this trap. If you find that you are letting other people control you just to keep the peace, then read on for some helpful information to get you back on track for total self-control. Check out some of the situations below and see if you find yourself in similar situations:

1. When people say mean things to you or speak harshly to you. And then you just walkway and never stand up for yourself. You hold all the pain inside, but you never let the other person know they have hurt you.

2. You never give your opinion on anything. You are worried that if you speak your mind and tell others were opinion, they may think you are foolish or laugh at you. If somebody wants to do something that you don't want to do, you just go along with them whether you enjoy it or not.

3. You always need people to give you consent or make you feel that it is okay before you take any action. You are an approval seeker. You are afraid to stand up and make a decision.

4. You live your life just going along with everybody else. You have no structure for your own life. You are willing to go along with anybody else's plan but have not got one of your own.

5. You have many goals and dreams; however, you do not dare to act on them. You find yourself saying I

can't do that. Because of this you live in fear of ever trying anything new.

6. You have many talents, but you are afraid to show your full potential. You find yourself going aimlessly through life and settling for less than you could be.

If any of the above statements sound true about you, then it is time for you to take control of your self and your life. You deserve better than to allow people to speak harshly to you. You deserve to stand up for yourself.

Your opinion is important, and you deserve to have it heard. You do not need other people's approval or consent in order to make a decision. Once you start making decisions on your own, you will start to feel better about yourself.

You deserve to have structure in your life and a plan of action to make your life more successful and enjoyable. You deserve to achieve your goals and dreams.

Never tell yourself that you can't do something. That is simply not true. If you can see something in your mind, then you have it within you to achieve it. Never be afraid to show people your full potential. Don't allow other people to control you and make you fearful of ever trying anything new. The more you get out and try new things and achieve the things that you have been avoiding, the better you will feel about yourself. You have the ability within you to do many great things. It's time to take control of yourself and become that person you know what is within you.

Understand and Get Control of Your Feelings

In order to get control of your feelings first you need to understand what makes you feel the way you do. You want to be able to understand why you handle any given situation the way you do. By knowing why you handle things the way you do you can have better control of yourself.

Try this simple exercise to help you understand your feeling;

Sit upright in a comfortable chair and pay close attention to how different parts of your body feel. Pay attention to how you breathe. Do you breathe in through your nose and out through your mouth? Is your breathing deep or shallow? Are there areas of your body feel tension? Just sit for a few minutes and become familiar with how your body reacts to sitting still in a chair.

Now pay close attention to any feelings, images or memories that come to your mind. What are these feelings telling you about yourself? Are you having positive or negative feelings? The more you get to understand your feelings, the more in touch with your emotions you become.

Take a few moments to acknowledge with feelings. If you are having bad feelings tell yourself it is okay to feel that at this time. Do not try to analyze your feelings right now. Just simply let your feelings come through. If you're feeling comfortable and at peace, just allow yourself to feel good.

If you are feeling the fear or anger, then allow yourself to discover what is causing this. If you're feeling pain, allow yourself to feel it and take note of what is causing the pain. Just let all your feelings come out and acknowledge them. By learning to understand your feelings, you can gain more self-control.

No matter what kind of feelings you are having, recognize that there is a reason for the way you are feeling. Gently ask yourself why you are feeling this way. Is there something happening that is making you feel this way? Was there a noise or scent that reminded you of something that made you feel that way?

Do not try to understand your feelings at this point. Try going deeper into your subconscious mind and see if you can reveal the reason for your feelings. The more you learn to recognize your feelings, the easier it is to figure out how to change them if needed.

Focus on the feeling you are having and express the feeling by making a sound that goes along with the feeling. You could scream, cry, take a deep breath; you could laugh or make any other sound that will express how you are feeling.

If you are feeling sad, you could reassure yourself by saying everything will be okay. Allow yourself to feel what ever emotion you are feeling and then comfort yourself. Allow yourself to totally recognize why you are feeling the way you are and then allow yourself to let go of the feeling. The more you get to know yourself, the more you will be able to achieve total self-control.

In Order to Gain Total Self Control First You Must Decide What You Want From Life

How would you describe your ideal life? What are your hopes and dreams? Are you looking for friends and relationships? Do you want more money and a better lifestyle? Do you wish you had better health? Would you like a better or more challenging job?

Have you ever tried to make changes to any of the areas of your life you wanted to change and were unable to succeed? What things did you do that made it not work out for you, and what do you think you could do differently to make it work now?

Maybe by taking a different approach than you did the first time you can succeed this time. Look at it from different angles and see if you can figure out ideas that will help you succeed this time.

No matter what it is that you want to do in order to have your ideal life, start working on the things it takes to make them happen. If you want better health, what changes would you need to make in order to make this happen? If you want to have more money, but you have negative thoughts about it, then try to change these thoughts to positive ones. If you would like a better job, what do you need to do in order to achieve this?

Take time to figure out all the different things you want and desire from your life and then write down everything you need to do in order to achieve these things. By knowing what you want out of life you are on your way to gaining self-control.

If you know what you want, then go after it with everything you've got. Develop a positive attitude towards reaching all your goals. Develop your skills each day and work on yourself and your confidence will grow.

You hold the key to your success within your hands. All you have to do is reach out and grab it. Take steps each day to work towards what you want out of life and each day will become a little easier and you will be a little closer to reaching your goals.

Develop These Qualities to Achieve Success

In order to get the success you desire in life you will need to work on your own personal development. Every time you attain a goal you will build your self-confidence, improve your relationships, and get closer to your financial goals and start feeling better about life in general.

Work on building these important skills and soon you will have more self-control

Decided now that you are going to be a more self-confident person. Tell yourself every day that you believe in yourself and that you know that you can achieve your goals in life. If you do not have self-confidence and do not believe in your self is very difficult to achieve total self-control. Tell your subconscious everyday that you are a self-confident person and that you know you can do anything you put your mind to.

Keep a positive attitude. When you have a negative and attitude it will get in your way every time. It will take away your energy and make you feel like you can not achieve your goals. If you allow yourself to be negative and say oh, I cannot do this, your subconscious mind will take over and say okay. Once this happens, it is very difficult to achieve what you want.

You have to tell yourself over and over again I can do it and then say what it is you want to do. Tell your subconscious I am going to do this, and I know I can do it. By repeating this consistently to your subconscious mind, it will have no choice but to believe it and make it so.

Learn how to communicate effectively with other people. There is nothing more important than learning how to communicate well with others. If you were in a room with 20 other people and told each one of them separately the exact same thing word for Word, every one of them would get something different out of it. This is why it's so important to learn how to communicate well. When you talk to others have them repeat back to you what you said and what they think you meant by that. This way you will be surer that they understood what you meant. Spend time on learning a proper tone of voice and how to use the right approach depending on who you are talking to.

Spend time learning new vocabulary and writing skills which will help you in your communication skills.

Learn how to manage stress. If you get stressed out every time something doesn't go your way, it will make it very difficult for you to achieve success. Spend time every day doing relaxation exercises in order to learn how to control stress better. The more you use stress relieving techniques the better you will become at meeting challenges that you face.

Do not let fear control your life. When you feel fear coming on, ask yourself is this a rational fear? If it is not, then tell yourself to let it go. Fear is an obstacle to reaching your goals. It can stop you from success by making you afraid to take the next step. Do not let it control you. You control it.

Accept Yourself and Realize Your Unique Self

If you're like many other people, you always try to please others in order to feel accepted. The problem with this is it can lead to you feeling depressed or unhappy. There is nothing wrong with caring about other people and trying to consider their feelings, however, if you are always miserable, then eventually people will want to be around you anyway.

You can take other people's feelings into consideration and still take care of yourself. You just need to find some kind of balance. By being yourself you are allowing yourself to be empowered. This will help you in every aspect of your life. You deserve to develop your potential and be yourself.

The first thing you need to do is get to know your self and what it is that you like. If you have always done what everybody else wanted, you may not even be sure what you really enjoy doing.

Take some time to pay attention to each thing you do during the week that somebody else wanted to do. Pay close attention as to whether you are enjoying yourself were not. If you find that you are unhappy or frustrated while doing these things, then the next time you are asked to go along, suggest something else or decline.

You may want to take a look at yourself in the mirror and get familiar with how you act, dress, walk, and talk. Is this the real you or are you behaving as you think others expect you to? You may want to ask a friend or family member to help you analyze your self. You may need a tough skin to handle what they have to say. Just make sure you find somebody who can be open and honest with you.

You are different than anybody else in the world. You have your own unique qualities that nobody else has.

When evaluating your personality, try to figure out if you have more negative or positive qualities. You need to learn how to accept yourself and remind yourself that you are a unique and special person. When you find negative aspects showing their ugly face, yell stop to your self and replace it with a positive.

You deserve others to respect you as well as you respecting yourself. Even if you have some bad qualities that you know you have, you realize that you can change them and that you deserve to be respected by others. Never allow yourself to be condemned by others and especially don't condemn yourself. If you find yourself doing this, remind yourself quickly that you are worthy of respect.

Once you understand what a wonderful and special person that you are, take time to get to know your self. Realize that by accepting yourself and showing respect towards yourself, every aspect of your life will be improved. You will have more self-confidence and self-esteem which in turn will make being in control of yourself much easier.

You Have the Right to Your Own Personal Power

Within each of us there is great power. Most people are unaware of this power. They feel that they are a victim in life and allow themselves to become powerless. Once you understand that you do have this great power within you, you can make changes in your life for the better.

It is up to you whether you use to power for good or evil. When you use it for good you will find every aspect of your life will become better. If you use it for evil you will destroy everything in your path and your life will become empty and sad.

You have it within you to generate your own personal power. You can use your emotions to believe in your own self-sufficiency and draw from your own inner strength in order to deal with everyday life.

If you do not use your own personal power you will find yourself letting other people use their power to control you. When this happens you allow other people to dominate you and control you and your life. The only thing this will do for you is make you feel powerless and therefore resent other people.

Take time to examine your actions. Do you find yourself always allowing others to run your life? Do you feel powerless, but you just keep taking it? Start today and realize that you have power and allow yourself to control your own life the way you want it to be. If other people try to control you, tell them you are no longer going to allow it and if they don't like it you're sorry but that's what has to be.

Take time to let go of beliefs that have been limiting you. It can be very difficult to change old habits but if you work on them a little at a time, it becomes easier each time.

The fact of the matter is that nobody is powerless. People that find themselves being controlled by others have usually started out by letting them get away with it once, and then it just kind of snowballs from there. Before you know it they just expect you to jump every time they ask you to. It becomes a habit to you as you feel powerless with this person. This is the pattern that must be broken and you must take your personal power back.

After you have allowed somebody to take your personal power away from you, you may find yourself trying to justify it. You may ask others to feel sorry for you because this person is controlling you.

If you catch yourself doing this, you have to stop immediately and walk away from the conversation. Then when you are alone write down exactly what happened and then analyze it to see how you can change the situation to gain control of your personal power again.

Once you break the wall down and quit letting people walk all over you, your life will start to take a change for the better. You will find that when you stand up for yourself your self-confidence will grow each time.

Your Potential and How to Keep It Under Your Control

Every person is unique and has an amazing amount of potential. When you are a child, you learned about your potential from your parents. As you grow and go to school you learn from teachers and other classmates.

You determined your potential based on how people treat you, how other people look, other peoples talent, if others are smarter than you or many other things. By the time you have grown up, you may have a false sense of your own potential based on some of these things.

Your potential is basically the things that you know you can do. By finding out the things that you are good at you are on your way to empowering yourself. Why not make a list of all of your talents and things that you are good at. It doesn't matter how small they are just keep writing until you've wrote everything that you know how to do. You will be amazed at how much potential you have that you haven't even been using.

Now that you have made the list of your talents, why not do some brainstorming and find ways to use these talents. Start out with a small list of ideas so you won't feel overwhelmed. Then work on one thing on your list until it is finished. You will get a sense of achievement by doing this and then you can move onto the next thing on your list. Once you have finished your first list, you can move on to a new list.

It is up to you to decide how much time you would like to spend working on your newfound potential. Just remember that the more you put in the more control you will have over your own life. You are the only one that can control your life. You can allow others to do it; however that is still you controlling your life. It is your decision to say, I am no longer going to let other people control me. I have the potential and the talent to control myself.

Believe In Your Self for Success

Do you believe that you are able to do anything you put your mind to? Are you aware that anything that you can think about or dream about, you have the power within you to achieve it? If you did not have the ability to achieve it, your mind would not be able to conceive of it. If there is something that you want to, but have been afraid to start, take baby steps if you have to, but start now.

Look at every change as an opportunity for growth. Every time you make the smallest change in your life you have the chance to grow and succeed in ways you never thought possible. Let go of old beliefs and replace them with new ones.

Most every belief you have has been programmed into your subconscious mind throughout your life by the way others treat you, or the way you allow others to treat you. It is up to you to form a new belief system and convince your subconscious mind that these things are true.

Once you have gotten rid of the old negative beliefs and replace them with positive beliefs, you will be more in control of your own life.

Learn how to question every certain belief you have held up to this time in your life. Take time to find out whether this is a truth or something that has been programmed in your mind which is untrue. Once you have changed your self limiting beliefs and have taken on new ones, you will see every aspect of your life starting to run more smoothly.

Your self-confidence will grow. You will become less pessimistic. You will become a more optimistic person. You will find achieving goals much easier. You will learn to accept yourself as a unique and special person. And your self-confidence will soar. Before you know it you will have total self-control.

ABSOLUTE CONCLUSION

- learning is applying -

"Learning without thinking is useless. Thought without learning is dangerous."

Kung Fu Tzu (Confucius)

I hope that all the knowledge acquired here is of benefit to you, leaving you one last piece of advice that you will surely see repeatedly throughout the book; The desire in conjunction with the plans and your goals are useless if you do not put the corresponding action with what you want to achieve.

Money is like the flow of a great river that emanates from a huge mountain, the flow of that river is inexhaustible and everyone, absolutely everyone, can drink from the river until they are satisfied, because there is enough, now to supply you and water all your crops alone You must concentrate and think about how to build a dam and a canal to divert part of the river flow to your lands.

It is very easy, simply if more money is needed in the world they will print part and the rest will be digitized, so don't worry, it doesn't matter if Jeff Bezos, Mark Zuckerberg, Jack Ma, Bill Gates, Warren Buffett, Larry Page , Elon Musk or Carlos Slim get richer every day, you can become richer than all of them together.

I wish you success and I encourage you to work on your level of thought and mental power, if you dare to start and leave the mass you will have a path of solidarity but in the end you will have to put security guards at the entrance of your house because people go to want to be with you for your money or because they want to learn from you, suddenly you will have many friends and relatives that you did not even know will appear, and most importantly, the most important thing is that you will have in your hands the decision and the power to teach others what you know and impact the world with a message and a legacy.

-/